First Steps

An ***LIRS GUIDE*** for Refugees, Asylum Seekers, and Migrants Released from Detention

Lutheran Immigration and Refugee Service

Edition 2014

For information or bulk orders, contact:
firststeps@lirs.org

LIRS.org

Printed by LIRS Press
Printed in the U.S.A.

International Standard Book Number: 978-0-9908689-4-1

DEDICATION

"This guide is dedicated to those who have fled persecution, torture, and violations of basic human rights and dignity. To the countless refugees, asylum seekers, survivors of torture and persecution, and migrants who have exercised courage most humans will never be able to comprehend: may you find safety, the freedom to direct your own lives, and a spirit of welcome here in America."

—*Angela Edman, LIRS Staff Attorney*

"To all the survivors out there, I want them to know that we are stronger and more resilient than we ever knew. We survived, that should be enough but it isn't. We must work hard to become whole again, to fill our soul with love and inspiration, to live the life that was intended for us before it was disrupted by war and horrors, and help rebuild a world that is better than the one we had just left."

—*Loung Ung, Cambodian-American Human Rights Activist*

Started by Lutheran congregations in 1939, Lutheran Immigration and Refugee Service (LIRS) is a national organization walking with migrants and refugees through ministries of service and justice, transforming U.S. communities by ensuring that newcomers are not only self-sufficient but also become connected and contributing members of their adopted communities in the United States.

PREFACE

By Selena Sujoldzic*

Home. It takes only four letters to write the word, but for some, it takes a lifetime to find its meaning. The word has caused me, as a former refugee, much pain, confusion, and uncertainty. When I finally found its meaning, I found peace. Home for me was Bosnia and Herzegovina. The bloody aggression and genocide inflicted upon Bosnia in the 1990s forced me and my family to run to save our lives. America opened its doors and welcomed us to its shores. With LIRS's help, we got back on our feet. My journey, as you will find with any former refugee, has been nothing short of interesting.

When my parents, older brother, and I resettled to America in 1995, I was 13 years old. We not only experienced culture shock, but we also did not know where to go from there. Lutheran church volunteers did all they could to help us, but we didn't know many of the basic steps we needed to take to begin our new lives. We didn't have a guide or a step-by-step explanation of how to build our future in a new country. My parents, who are chemical engineers and are well-educated people, felt helpless and unable to guide their two teenaged children out of this confusing time.

We encountered many roadblocks; some were presented by life itself, and some by people who did not accept us. Only through true resilience did we overcome these obstacles and gain the ability to call America our home. My fellow migrants: you too will encounter obstacles and people who will not accept you. You will be judged by the community, as well as by people who come from the same place as you. This is inescapable. You must remember one thing: you are in America now, where the only person who can stand in your way is you. Other roadblocks and people can stop you only if you let them. That is the beauty of this country. You have the freedom to shape your own life and build your own future.

Be proud of where you come from. Respect your culture and remember your heritage. Then take all of that pride and respect and use it to move forward in this great country. Do not miss opportunities by remaining stuck in the past and the "what-ifs." When I let go of my past, my present came to light and suddenly, I had a future.

I wish that my family and I had a guide like *First Steps* to tell us how to move forward and take advantage of America's great opportunities; what benefits were available to us; where we could turn for help and find legal, social, medical, and community resources; and what important laws and procedures we needed to understand and utilize. I am certain if we had, we would have started calling this country "home" much sooner, and spent fewer years living in uncertainty. We spent enough time living in uncertainty and darkness in our birth countries, and no one should have to live that way here too.

Finally, just as it is important to be proud of where you come from, it is also important to feel American. It does not mean you are forgetting your heritage; it simply means you have a place you can once again call home. We come from a place where other people got to write our books of life and dictate our faith. America is giving you a chance to start over, a chance to write your own book of life. I am still writing mine; it includes all my mistakes, all my regrets, all my successes; but it's MINE. From this day forward, start writing the chapters of your book of life. I hope *First Steps* can be part of your first chapter, and will guide you to a place where you will no longer feel like a refugee, but a person who can smile and say, "I am home."

** Selena Sujoldzic is a former refugee from Bosnia and Herzegovina, and arrived in the U.S. in 1995. She earned her law degree, and is now a practicing attorney in Wichita, Kansas. Selena has been a leader in LIRS's Refugee Academy, an opportunity for former refugees to build advocacy, community organizing, and leadership skills. She hopes to use her experience as a refugee and her law degree to help others like her.*

WELCOME

If you have recently been released from immigration detention: this guide will help you find support and assistance while you build a new life in the United States (U.S.). If you fled from your home country to seek protection in the U.S., this guide will help you find legal and community support during the last part of your journey to safety. If you are a lawyer, case manager, or otherwise provide services to newcomers, this guide may help you find information that will empower your clients to understand and access their rights.

This guide aims to provide information and resources to help you make your way from your home country, possibly through immigration detention, to a situation of safety and security in the U.S. It provides very important information on your rights, responsibilities, and eligibility for basic services and benefits such as healthcare, education, and other necessities. It also provides information on community and cultural groups to help you feel at home in America. It has many details, so if you do not understand something, take it to your lawyer or case manager, and ask them to explain it to you.

Because a lot of these rights depend on why you came to the U.S.

and what type of legal status you have or are seeking, we have expanded our previous version of *First Steps,* published in 2005 under its previous title, *Pocket Knowledge,* to include not only more in-depth and updated information, but also have added detailed information according to immigration status. This guide provides information about rights, responsibilities, services, and benefits in general, and provides specific information for those who fled to the U.S. to escape persecution or torture in their home countries, including: refugees, asylees, asylum seekers, and those seeking withholding of removal or protection under the Convention Against Torture. Lutheran Immigration and Refugee Service (LIRS) is releasing supplements covering other statuses, and this guide may already contain some of these supplements. More information on statuses, and how to obtain information for those holding or seeking other statuses, can be found in Chapter 2.

Please note that this guide provides information about the law; however, you should always consult with a lawyer if you have legal questions. Do not rely on this guide instead of seeking the advice of a lawyer. In Chapter 3, you will find information about how to find a lawyer. Be sure to ask a lawyer or a resettlement agency for help with your questions, especially if your case is still pending and even if you have already won your case.

This guide lists many other phone numbers to help you. The final section provides directories of Resettlement Agencies for refugees, torture treatment programs, immigration legal services providers, and other important phone numbers and websites.

It is important to know that the U.S. immigration system is always changing. The Department of Homeland Security (DHS) is the federal agency that oversees immigration. Within DHS, U.S. Citizenship and Immigration Services (USCIS) is in charge of

WELCOME

immigration services; Immigration and Customs Enforcement (ICE) enforces immigration laws within the U.S., and Customs and Border Protection (CBP) enforces immigration laws at the border. The Executive Office of Immigration Review (EOIR) is within the Department of Justice (DOJ), and is in charge of the immigration court system. The information in this guide may change. Call the phone numbers listed to get current information.

If you are a provider of legal, social, medical, or community services, please utilize this guide to help your clients find more detailed information and resources. You may wish to distribute the shorter status-specific supplements to your clients, and use this longer guide as a reference. Please also share with other service providers.

If you are a church or faith-based organization, please also use this guide to help migrants you serve understand their rights, and distribute any relevant status-specific supplements to migrants. Please share the supplements and the link to this guide with other churches and religious groups, ethnic community groups, and organizations in your communities and networks, particularly those which attract asylum seekers and migrants. Please also assist us in distributing the link and supplements to homeless shelters, colleges, and other institutions or organizations in your communities that may attract asylum seekers and migrants. You may contact us for more copies.

First Steps has been brought to you by the Detained Torture Survivors' Legal Support Network, a program of LIRS's Access to Justice Unit.

First Steps is available online at www.lirs.org/firststeps. Please go to the website to view updates. This guide was accurate as of August 2014 but note that the accuracy of this information may change over time.

FIRST STEPS

If you have any questions, concerns, or comments about *First Steps,* please email firststeps@lirs.org.

We hope that you will find *First Steps* useful and share it with others.

Good luck!

CONTENTS

SECTION ONE: Introduction and Important Information

17 Chapter 1—Important General Tips

SECTION TWO: Legal Rights and Responsibilities

25 Chapter 2—Statuses: Refugees, Asylees, and Asylum Seekers
35 Chapter 3—Legal Services and Immigration Court
43 Chapter 4—What are the Immigration Consequences of Criminal Convictions?
51 Chapter 5—What are Your Rights If You Have Been Arrested?
59 Chapter 6—How to Get Your Personal Property After You Are Released From Detention
63 Chapter 7—Case Status and Proof of Status
69 Chapter 8—What You Must Do When You Change Your Address
73 Chapter 9—How to Reunite Your Family
77 Chapter 10—How to Get Your Green Card (Adjustment of Status)
87 Chapter 11—How to Become a U.S. Citizen
101 Chapter 12—Traveling Outside of the United States
105 Chapter 13—Voting, the Selective Service Requirement, and Joining the Military
109 Chapter 14—Right to Work

SECTION THREE: Basic Services and Needs

115 Chapter 15—How to Get a Work Permit: Employment Authorization Document (EAD)
129 Chapter 16—How to Get a Social Security Number
137 Chapter 17—How to Get a State ID Card
141 Chapter 18—How to Get Public Benefits and Financial Support
165 Chapter 19—How to Access Health Care
181 Chapter 20–How to Access Housing
187 Chapter 21—How to Access Education and Childcare

SECTION FOUR: Integration, Interpersonal Connections, and Community Support

195 Chapter 22—How to Keep Your Money Safe and Make It Grow
207 Chapter 23—How to Get Emotional Support
213 Chapter 24—Religious, Cultural, and Community Groups
217 Chapter 25—Directory of Resettlement Agencies (RAs)
219 Chapter 26—Directory of National Consortium of Torture Treatment Programs
249 Chapter 27—Directory of Immigration Legal Services Providers
277 Chapter 28—Other Important Phone Numbers and Websites

CONTENTS

281 Glossary
293 Acknowledgments

Important Deadline:

If you were granted asylum, refugee status, SIV status, or a T-visa in the last 31 days and are not yet participating in the Matching Grant Program, or your state's equivalent, please go directly to Chapter 18, "How to Get Public Benefits and Financial Support." This opportunity to sign up for valuable help expires after 31 days!

SECTION 1

Introduction and Important Information

CHAPTER 1

Important General Tips

There is a Glossary at the back of *First Steps* which may help you to understand some of the words in this guide.

Ask for Help

If you have questions about anything, ask someone you trust for help. This might be a family member, a close friend, your lawyer, your case manager, or your religious leader.

What to Do in an Emergency

If you have an emergency, dial 911 on any phone.

An emergency includes any situation that poses an immediate threat to someone's life, physical health, or personal property. The operator who answers will ask you for information about the emergency. Then the operator will contact the fire department, police, or hospital to help you. You will not need to give your name or any personal information when you call about an emergency. You will only need to give the address where the emergency is happening.

Poison Control

Many things in your home can be poisonous if they are swallowed. These can include cleaning products, medicine, paint, alcohol, cosmetics, and even some plants. Keep these things away from young children. **If someone swallows a poisonous substance, call the Poison Control Center right away at 1-800-222-1222.** You can get help 24 hours a day, seven days a week. Have the poisonous substance with you when you call. Tell the operator what it is. If you do not speak English, tell the operator so an interpreter can help you. Calls to the Poison Control Center are confidential and free.

Privacy and Identity Safety

Important! Your social security number, identification documents, financial records and court records are private. Only share these documents with people you trust, and/or a professional who is working directly on your case.

How to Make a Phone Call

You can find a list of important phone numbers in Chapter 28, "Important Phone Numbers and Websites."

- A phone number is 10 digits, for example (123)-456-7890. The first three digits are the area code. The area code tells you where in the country the person is calling from. If you are calling from a landline (not a mobile phone) in some areas, you may also need to dial a "1" before the 10-digit number, if you are in a different area code than the number you are calling. When using mobile phones, just dial the 10 digits, no matter where you are calling in the U.S. Ask someone how the phone system works in your area.

- Toll-free phone numbers are free. The person you are calling pays the charges. 1-800, 1-888, 1-877, 1-866, 1-855 are all area codes for toll-free calls.

- Collect calls are also free, but only if the person you are calling agrees to pay for the call. To make a collect call, dial "0" before the area code instead of "1" (for example, 0-123-456-7890). The operator will ask you for your name, and will ask the person you are calling if they are willing to accept the call (and pay the charge).

- To find a phone number, look in a phone book called the "white pages" for homes or the "yellow pages" for businesses. The local phone company provides phone books to each home, business and public library. If you cannot find a phone book, you can call 411 for help but you may be charged for the call. You can also go online to www.whitepages.com or www.yellowpages.com.

Whenever you meet someone new, you can ask them for their business card. A business card is a piece of paper with a person's name and phone number.

Appointments are the way many people and businesses in the U.S. make plans. Be on time for all appointments. If you think you might be even five minutes late, call the person you are going to meet. This will show respect to the person. It will also help them respect you.

How to Send Mail

Post offices are places where you send and receive mail. Ask someone where the nearest post office is. You will use the post office to send many of the important forms discussed in this guide. Be sure you always request a return receipt when you send out your immigration forms. A return receipt will cost a small fee, but assures that you will receive a postcard in the mail as proof that the government official received your mail. Keep this postcard with the copies of your important documents.

At the post office, you can also pay to have a post office (P.O.) box where you receive mail if you do not have a stable home address.

Public Library

Public libraries are a helpful resource. They have a wide collection of books, movies, newspapers, and magazines. All materials are free and available for everyone to use in the library. If you would like to borrow a resource, or take it home for a few days, you must apply for a free library card. Generally, to be eligible for a library card you must show proof that you live in or own property in the state where the library is located. To apply you must show identification with your name, signature, and current address. Most libraries will accept a combination of documents such as; valid driver's license, valid state identification, passport, utility bill or lease document dated within the past thirty days, current employee identification, etc. Ask your local librarian for more details, as every library is different. Libraries often offer community classes and literacy programs. Ask for a list of programs and classes the library offers.

Many libraries offer free computer and internet access. If you do not have an email account, go to one of the following websites to set one up: www.yahoo.com, www.gmail.com, or www.hotmail.com. The library staff can help show you how to use the computer and the internet.

IMPORTANT GENERAL TIPS

Parks & Recreation

Local parks provide picnic areas, playgrounds, and sports fields to the public. Many parks have regulations about what visitors can and cannot do. Some parks are free, but others charge an admission fee. Parks are a great place to get exercise and a great way to get out of your home.

Religious Organizations and Community Centers

Visiting religious organizations and community centers are a great way to meet people in your community, make connections, and learn about resources available in your neighborhood. Use the phone book or internet to research local centers, or ask your neighbors or library staff. See Chapter 24, "Religious, Cultural, and Community Groups," for more resources.

Important Government Agencies

Immigration benefits, such as permission to remain and work in the U.S., are provided by the U.S. Citizenship and Immigration Services ("USCIS") and the immigration courts (sometimes called "EOIR," which stands for Executive Office of Immigration Review.) USCIS and EOIR are agencies of the U.S. government. Applying for immigration benefits can be difficult, and not everyone who applies for the benefits will get them. Many legal service agencies and law firms have immigration experts who can help you decide whether you qualify for benefits. If you qualify, the experts can help you complete the forms. Work with immigration experts whenever possible. For more information, read Chapter 3, "Legal Services and Immigration Court."

These government websites may be useful:

- U.S. Citizenship and Immigration Services (USCIS): www.uscis.gov

- Office of Refugee Resettlement (ORR): www.acf.hhs.gov/programs/orr
- Social Security Administration (SSA): www.ssa.gov

Obeying the Law

There can be very serious consequences if you are caught breaking the law in the U.S. Not only can you go to jail, **but many crimes in the U.S. that may not seem serious can get you deported.** Some acts that are not illegal in other countries may be illegal in the U.S. Some examples of illegal acts in the U.S. are physically harming a child or spouse, following someone who does not want to be followed, or having sexual interactions with a person under the age of 18 if you are older. If you are not sure, ask! Read more about how your immigration case and status can be affected by criminal activity in Chapter 4.

Important! Keep with you at all times the name and phone number of a lawyer who can help you. If you need to find a lawyer, call one of the following phone numbers:

- AILA (American Immigration Lawyers Association) Immigration Lawyer Referral Service: www.ailalawyer.com, (202-216-2400)
- National Lawyers Guild, National Immigration Project: www.nationalimmigrationproject.org, (617-227-9727)
- Immigration Law Help: www.immigrationlawhelp.org (search by state)
- EOIR Free Legal Service Provider List: www.justice.gov/eoir/probono/states.htm (search by state)

SECTION 2

Legal Rights and Responsibilities

CHAPTER 2

Immigrants Covered in This Guide: Those Who Have Received Protection from Persecution or Torture, and Those Who Currently Seek It

Statuses: Refugees, Asylees, Asylum Seekers, Withholding of Removal, Withholding under the Convention Against Torture (CAT), and Deferral under CAT

This guide contains information specific to two general groups of people fleeing persecution or torture in their home countries:

1. Those who have sought protection from persecution and have **already been granted status** as a **refugee** or **asylee,** and
2. Those who are **currently seeking asylum ("asylum seekers").**

Important Note: This guide also contains specific information for those who have been granted or who seek "withholding of removal," and those who have been granted or who seek protection under the Convention Against Torture (CAT). This is because withholding of removal is a lesser form of protection that asylum seekers can and generally should apply for at the same time they seek asylum, to increase their protection options. Similarly, asylum seekers who have experienced torture should also apply for protection under CAT while applying for asylum.

Information about these groups is below, and specific information for each of these statuses is included in the chapters that cover topics related to rights or benefits specific to status.

Important Note: This guide contains information that is applicable to migrants in any status (or without any status at all), so if you do not fit under one of the above-named categories, you can still use this guide for information. However, LIRS plans to release status-specific supplements to this guide for those who are seeking or have the following statuses:

- Asylum seekers
- LPRs (lawful permanent residents, or those with green cards),
- Victim of Trafficking, or T-visa (Trafficking visa),
- U-visa (immigrant victims of crime in the U.S.),
- VAWA (protection under the Violence Against Women Act as a battered spouse or child of a U.S. citizen or legal permanent resident, or battered parent of a U.S. citizen),
- SIJS (Special Immigrant Juvenile Status),
- Possible other status-specific supplements as needed in the future.

The following sections provide information about the statuses covered in this publication.

STATUSES: REFUGEES, ASYLEES, AND ASYLUM SEEKERS

What is a Refugee?

You are a refugee if you cannot return to your home country because you have suffered past persecution or have a well-founded fear of future persecution based on your race, religion, nationality, political opinion, or membership in a particular social group; and your government is unwilling or unable to protect you.

The term "refugee" refers to those who have already proven this fear and had their status as refugees approved in another country, by the United Nations High Commissioner for Refugees (UNHCR) or another international or government body, and have already been resettled as refugees in the U.S.

Refugees can eventually become U.S. citizens, and have many rights and access to benefits, which are explained in detail in this guide.

What is an Asylee?

An asylee, like a refugee, is someone who cannot return to his home country because of past persecution or a well-founded fear of future persecution based on race, religion, nationality, political opinion, or membership in a particular social group, and his government is unwilling or unable to protect him.

The term "asylee" refers to those who have had their statuses approved in the U.S., by either an asylum officer at USCIS or an Immigration Judge in court. In contrast, refugees have been resettled after having their statuses approved abroad.

Asylees can eventually become U.S. citizens, and have many rights and access to benefits, which are explained in detail in this guide.

What is an Asylum Seeker?

If you are an asylum seeker you have (1) applied for asylum, (2) indicated a plan to apply for asylum, or (3) indicated an intent to apply for withholding of removal (WOR). Asylum is a form of protection available to people who meet the definition of a refugee, but are already in the U.S. If you are applying for asylum, you must prove that you are fearful of returning home, meaning you have suffered past persecution or are in fear of future persecution in your home country because of your race, religion, nationality, political opinion, or membership in a particular social group.

You can apply "affirmatively," with USCIS (U.S. Citizenship and Immigration Services) *only* if you came into the U.S. legally on another type of visa, or were paroled at a point of entry, and are not in removal proceedings in court. You will submit an application and be interviewed by an Asylum Officer. You must apply "defensively" with an Immigration Judge in court if you are in removal proceedings, either because you entered the U.S. without a valid visa and were likely placed in immigration detention until passing a credible fear interview (discussed below), you were arrested for a crime, or your immigration status expired.

To apply for asylum, you must file Form I-589, Application for Asylum and for Withholding of Removal, located at: www.uscis.gov/i-589. You will answer questions about your identity, history, family, and reasons you left your country. You will write a "personal declaration" that focuses on why you left your country and why you fear returning, and that shows how you fit into the refugee definition. You will be asked to provide evidence or documentation of your identity and the persecution you have suffered or that you fear.

It is highly recommended that you consult an immigration attorney for help with applying for asylum, because the application process is very complicated, and your chances of success are much higher with an immigration attorney. This is especially true if you have an arrest or criminal record. A list of immigration legal services providers organized by state appears at the end of this guide. **If you cannot find a lawyer, please see the Florence Immigrant and Refugee Rights Project's guide on how to apply for asylum, at** http://www.firrp.org/media/Asylum_WOR_CAT-Guide-2013.pdf.

Note: Immigration Detention for Asylum Seekers and Credible/ Reasonable Fear Interviews

Unless you entered the U.S. on a valid visa, you were likely arrested at the border or a port of entry to the U.S., and placed in immigration detention to wait for a "credible fear interview" (CFI), in which an asylum officer asks basic questions to determine whether it is possible you have a real fear of being persecuted if returned to your home country. If you were previously removed and came back to the U.S., were ordered removed but never left, or were convicted of an aggravated felony, you will undergo a similar process called a "reasonable fear interview" (RFI), but you must wait longer for that.

Those who pass their interview must then apply for asylum "defensively" in immigration court. It is important to remember that asylum seekers who pass their interview have not been granted asylum; they have been given the *chance to apply* for asylum, and are still in removal proceedings.

If you do not pass your CFI or RFI, you may appeal to an Immigration Judge. If the judge disagrees with the asylum officer and decides there *is* the possibility of persecution upon return to your home country, you will be allowed to proceed with your application. If the judge decides that you do not have a credible or reasonable fear of persecution, you will be returned to immigration officials for removal. There is no appeal of the judge's decision.

If you were arrested while entering the U.S. at a port of entry and passed your interview, you may request release "on parole," which means you are asking the government to release you from detention while your immigration case goes forward. You must have identification documents, and must show immigration authorities that you have a sponsor or tie in the community who will agree to provide food and shelter if you are released; that you will show up to all your immigration hearings in court; and that you are not a danger to the community. Unfortunately, there is no way to appeal a negative parole decision. However, if you have been detained for longer than six months, contact an immigration attorney.

If you were arrested somewhere other than a port of entry to the U.S., have not been convicted of certain crimes, and passed your credible or reasonable fear interview, you may request release on bond. You are requesting that an Immigration Judge release you from detention while your immigration case goes forward, and allow you (or a sponsor) to pay a "bond," or a large sum of money to guarantee you will show up to your immigration hearings if you are released. If you show up to your hearings and obey the judge's order, the bond will be returned when the case is over. You must convince the judge you are not a danger to the community, and that you will show up to your immigration court hearings. If your bond request is rejected, you may appeal.

STATUSES: REFUGEES, ASYLEES, AND ASYLUM SEEKERS

For more information, see the Florence Project's bond guide, at www.firrp.org/media/Bond-Guide-2013.pdf. For information on appealing a negative bond decision, see the Florence Project's guide on appeals, *Appealing Your Case to the Board of Immigration Appeals,* starting at page 12 for bond appeals, at www.firrp.org/media/BIA-Appeal-Guide-2013.pdf.

Many asylum seekers wish to be released as soon as possible, as it is easier to find a lawyer and focus the case without having to deal with the stresses of detention. However, some prefer to stay in detention, because cases for detained asylum seekers move more quickly than for those who have been released.

If you are not sure what to do, or have been waiting for your CFI for more than 14 days, ask immigration detention officials for the list of free or low-cost immigration lawyers, and contact one. Unfortunately, those awaiting RFIs must often wait several months.

For more information on the credible and reasonable fear processes, see the Florence Project's *Guide to Credible & Reasonable Fear Proceedings* at www.firrp.org/media/CF-RF-Guide-2013.pdf.

<u>What Can Make You Ineligible for Asylum</u>

Important! You must file for asylum within one year of entering the U.S. If you have been in the U.S. for more than one year, you are not eligible for asylum! There are only two exceptions to this rule, and they are very hard to achieve: circumstances in your country must have changed such that you are now at risk for new or increased persecution, or there were extraordinary circumstances that kept you from applying within one year (for instance, hiring an attorney who failed to file your case, or having a life-threatening illness.) If you missed your deadline, you should see an attorney for help.

You will be **ineligible** for asylum if you missed the one-year filing deadline (with the few exceptions mentioned above); have committed or been convicted of an aggravated felony; have committed or been convicted of a "particularly serious crime" in the U.S. and are a danger to the community; have strong ties to another country and have been firmly resettled there; have ever persecuted another person based on their race, religion, nationality, political opinion, or particular social group; have committed a serious, non-political crime in your country; or are considered a terrorist or otherwise dangerous to the U.S.

You have limited rights and access to benefits while you are an asylum seeker. Details are provided in this guide. If your application is approved, you become an asylee.

What is Withholding of Removal?

Withholding of Removal is a form of relief similar to asylum, but with fewer rights. To win withholding, you must prove you are "more likely than not" to suffer persecution in your home country on account of your race, religion, nationality, political opinion, or membership in a particular social group. To apply, you must fill out form I-589, Application for Asylum and Withholding of Removal, located at www.uscis.gov/i-589. Most people apply for asylum and withholding at the same time. However, Asylum Officers cannot grant withholding; only Immigration Judges can, so your status will be decided in immigration court. It is highly recommended that you seek a lawyer's help.

Withholding is a lesser form of protection than asylum, so you may be granted withholding of removal if you are ineligible for asylum because you missed the one-year filing deadline, or had a criminal conviction that disqualifies you for asylum, like an aggravated felony. Certain crimes also may make you ineligible to receive withholding, but the requirements are less strict. For example, if you were convicted of an aggravated felony and sentenced to less than five years, you will be ineligible for asylum, but may still be eligible for withholding. However, if you were sentenced to more than five years for a very serious crime, you will not be eligible for either.

Withholding of removal allows you to stay in the U.S. instead of being deported, and provides some rights, like the right to work and receive some health benefits. However, you can never apply for a green card or U.S. citizenship and cannot bring your family. Details of your eligibility for other benefits are in this guide.

In this guide, withholding of removal may also be referred to as "withholding under the INA," in contrast to "withholding under CAT," which is explained below. ("INA" stands for "Immigration and Nationality Act," which is the large body of law that governs immigration in the U.S.)

What Does Withholding or Deferral Under the Convention Against Torture (CAT) Mean?

Foreign citizens who have been tortured or who fear torture by their government in their home country can apply for protection under CAT. This is a form of protection that prevents the government from deporting you back to a country where you are likely to be tortured. Unlike asylum and withholding, the torture does not have to be for reasons related to your race, religion, nationality, political opinion, or membership in a particular social group.

Like withholding, CAT is a lesser form of protection than asylum. You may be eligible to apply for a work permit, and will not be deported as long as you face torture in your home country, but you can never apply for a green card or U.S. citizenship, cannot bring your family, and have limited rights, which are detailed in this guide.

Some of these rights depend on which type of protection you receive. There are two types of protection under CAT:

1. Withholding of removal under CAT: also referred to as "withholding under CAT," offers more protection and more rights, and you will receive this type if you have not been convicted of a particularly serious crime. You can only lose your status if DHS reopens your case and proves you no longer face torture in your home country.
2. Deferral under CAT: this is a more temporary form of protection against deportation that is granted if you likely face torture, but are ineligible for asylum, withholding under the INA, or withholding under CAT because you were convicted of a particularly serious crime; are accused of terrorism, persecution, or other international crimes; or are otherwise a danger to the U.S. Your status will end when the government can show you are no longer likely to face torture, and the government may detain you until that point. You have very limited rights, which are detailed in this guide.

CHAPTER 3

Legal Services and Immigration Court

If you are being released from immigration detention, it is important for you to know what legal services are available to you. Legal service providers are people you can go to for advice about your immigration case. They can tell you what immigration benefits you are eligible for and can apply for. You may see a lawyer (also called an attorney), or a representative accredited by the Board of Immigration Appeals (BIA), which will be explained below. Applying for immigration benefits can be difficult. Many legal services providers have immigration experts who can help you understand whether you qualify for immigration benefits. If you qualify, the experts can help you complete the forms. These legal experts can also help represent you if your immigration case is still pending.

What are Immigration Court Proceedings?

If you are in deportation or removal proceedings, the U.S. government is trying to remove you from the U.S. The government will be represented by an Immigration and Customs Enforcement (ICE) attorney, who will argue that you do not have a legal right to remain in the U.S. It is hard for anyone without a law degree to represent themselves against a trained ICE attorney, especially for people from other countries.

This is why it is very important that you try to find an immigration lawyer who can represent you in court. Your lawyer will ask you questions about your background, history, and why you came to the U.S. It is very important that you tell your lawyer the truth and answer all of your lawyer's questions fully, because your lawyer will use the information you give to determine what kind of legal relief you are eligible for. ("Legal relief" here means what kind of status or visa you might be eligible for, depending on your circumstances; such as asylum or another protection-related status.) Your lawyer will then argue that you are eligible to stay in the U.S., based on the type of legal relief your lawyer determines you are eligible for.

What Can I Do If My Rights Were Violated in Immigration Court Proceedings?

If you have a complaint about how an Immigration Judge treated you in court, and believe there may have been abuse, mistreatment, discrimination, or other types of violations, you may write a letter to the Executive Office for Immigration Review (EOIR), which is the division of the Department of Justice that operates the immigration court system. *Do not* submit a complaint if you simply disagree with the judge's opinion.

Include your name, your A-number, your contact information, the name of the judge, the date and location of the event, and a description of what happened. You may submit your complaint by email to EOIR.IJConduct@usdoj.gov, or you may mail the complaint to the Assistant Chief Immigration Judge for Conduct and Professionalism or the appropriate supervisory Assistant Chief Immigration Judge (ACIJ). You can find the contact information for the ACIJ in charge of your court system or issue at www.justice.gov/eoir/sibpages/ACIJAssignments.htm.

How to Find Legal Services

Be careful. Some people say they are experts, but instead charge you a lot of money and do not provide help for your case. They may even harm your case. Make sure the person helping you is either an immigration lawyer or a BIA accredited representative (explained below).

You can go online to www.uscis.gov/avoidscams for tips on how to avoid seeking help from people who are not experts. You can also check www.justice.gov/eoir/discipline.htm for a list of lawyers who have been disciplined by EOIR for bad practice of immigration law. You can also check with your state's bar association (which allows lawyers to practice) to make sure your lawyer is licensed and has not been disciplined for bad practice.

What to Do If You Have Been the Victim of Immigration Fraud or Scams, or Poor Lawyering

If you have been the victim of immigration fraud or scams, you should submit a report to the Federal Trade Commission at www.ftccomplaintassistant.gov/#crnt&panel1-1. Also see USCIS's page on reporting scams, to find out where to report the fraud in your state, at www.uscis.gov/avoid-scams/report-immigration-scams. Make copies of these reports, and after you find a new lawyer, take the records to your new lawyer.

If you saw a lawyer who made a mistake, failed to file something on time, or failed to correctly advise you on your case, you may be able to take steps with a new lawyer to save your case. It is always helpful to keep your own records, including copies of documents

For a list of free or low-cost immigration legal service providers in your state, please visit the following websites:

- **AILA (American Immigration Lawyers Association) Immigration Lawyer Referral Service:** www.ailalawyer.com, (202-216-2400)
- **National Lawyers Guild, National Immigration Project:** www.nationalimmigrationproject.org, (617-227-9727)
- **Immigration Law Help:** www.immigrationlawhelp.org (search by state)
- **EOIR Free Legal Services Provider List:** www.justice.gov/eoir/probono/states.htm (search by state)

you gave to your lawyer, records of visits and phone calls, filings made (or filings your lawyer promised to make), and receipts for money you paid your lawyer. If you have any of these, bring them to your new lawyer. He or she may be able to help you file an "ineffective assistance of counsel" claim, which shows that you took all the proper steps to file your case, but that a previous lawyer made mistakes. If successful, you will be allowed to proceed with your case.

There are different ways to find an expert to help with your immigration case. Many organizations provide free or low-cost representation to immigrants who cannot afford a lawyer.

You can also view a list of lawyers, listed by state, in Chapter 27, "Directory of Immigration Legal Services Providers," and a list of general resources, including organizations that can help you find legal services for your specific needs, in Chapter 28, "Important Phone Numbers and Websites."

You should visit the USCIS website's page on finding legal services at www.uscis.gov/avoid-scams/find-legal-services. It includes information on finding a lawyer and on finding a BIA accredited representative. "BIA" stands for "Board of Immigration Appeals," which is the highest part of the U.S. immigration court system, where parties to an immigration case can appeal if they don't agree with an Immigration Judge's decision. The BIA also accredits certain organizations and people who are not lawyers, but are experts on immigration, to answer certain immigration questions and help fill out immigration forms. Most BIA accredited organizations can help you for a lower fee than a lawyer. You can find a list of BIA accredited organizations near you by visiting www.justice.gov/eoir/ra/raroster.htm and clicking "Recognized Organizations List." You can also find BIA accredited organizations by calling your local Resettlement Agency (see Chapter 25, "Directory of Resettlement Agencies [RAs]").

If you cannot find an immigration expert, you can use the *pro se* materials developed by Florence Immigrant and Refugee Rights Project. *"Pro se"* means to represent yourself in court, instead of using a lawyer. The *pro se* packets will explain how to apply for immigration benefits by yourself or represent yourself in court. You can find the packets on the Florence Project website at www.firrp.org.

You can also find materials that explain if you might qualify for immigration benefits, such as permission to work in the U.S., and how you can apply. You can get more information and find immigration forms in one of the following ways:

- Call USCIS at 1-800-870-3676 and request the appropriate forms.
- Get the forms from the USCIS website on the Internet at www.uscis.gov/forms.
- Call the USCIS National Customer Service Center at 1-800-375-5283 with questions about immigration forms.

Important! Make sure that you get your immigration forms from USCIS. Many non-USCIS websites offer immigration forms, some of which may be fake and designed to trick you into giving money. Even if they are providing legitimate forms, non-USCIS sites may not have the current versions of the forms. USCIS may deny or delay your petition if you use outdated forms. You may even lose the money you paid in fees and have to pay again when you submit the correct form.

Following Your Case

It is very important that you follow the status of your immigration case if it is still pending. Failure to show up in court or follow the immigration process will harm your ability to get legal protective status to stay in the U.S. If you have a case in Immigration Court, check the date of your next hearing, case status, or other information by calling the Executive Office for Immigration Review's Case Information System at **240-314-1500** or **1-800-898-7180.** You will need your A-number.

You can check the status of your asylum or other applications before USCIS at **https://egov.uscis.gov/cris/Dashboard/CaseStatus.do**, or call the USCIS National Customer Service Center at **1-800-375-5283**. This is an automated system. That means you will not talk to a person. You will get information on your case by pressing numbers on the phone. You will need your A-number, any receipt number issued by Immigration, and the last notice you received about your case on the phone. Your A-number is an 8-digit or 9-digit number that starts with A. It is written on all of your immigration papers. The Service Center provides specific information about the status of an individual application by phone if you electronically filed, or filed at a Service Center and have a receipt/tracking number. Otherwise, use the online system.

CHAPTER 4

What Are the Immigration Consequences of Criminal Convictions?

Interacting with the U.S. criminal justice system is always a stressful experience. Noncitizens face additional challenges since the outcome of their criminal proceedings can affect their immigration status, even leading to their removal from the U.S. Fortunately, immigrants have a constitutional right to know if a criminal plea will have immigration consequences. The following information will help you exercise this important right, as well as provide other guidance. This guidance is not meant to replace legal advice and you should talk to an immigration lawyer if you have specific questions about your case.

What to Know Before Dealing with Criminal Issues

MYTH: Because the U.S. has given me refugee/asylee status, they would never send me back to the same country where I was persecuted, no matter what.

CHAPTER 4

FACT: The U.S. regularly strips people of their immigration status and removes them to their country of citizenship, even if they are/were refugees or asylees, often as a result of criminal convictions. Even a minor offense like shoplifting could result in your removal from the U.S. Therefore, it is important to exercise your right to be informed about the immigration consequences of any potential criminal pleas or convictions.

MYTH: If I have lawful permanent resident (LPR) status, I can't be removed from the U.S.

FACT: LPR status is not always "permanent." Thousands of immigrants with LPR status, including refugees and asylees, are removed each year because of criminal convictions. Unless you have obtained U.S. citizenship, you could be removed because of a criminal conviction.

MYTH: Since the U.S. is not actually sending people back to my country of origin, it doesn't really matter if I am ordered removed or not.

FACT: It is true that at any given time, the U.S. may not be physically able to remove people to their country of citizenship because of war, problems in diplomatic relations, natural disasters, or other reasons. This is *not* a permanent guarantee of safety. At any time the U.S. might be able to remove you and you will have to leave the U.S., sometimes in as little as two weeks. Even if the U.S. does not physically remove you, living with an order of removal is difficult. You have to check in with Immigration on a regular basis and if you fail to do so, you could be detained. You will have to apply and pay for a separate work authorization document. You will also lose important rights such as the right to bring family members into the U.S. or receive certain federal benefits.

WHAT ARE THE IMMIGRATION CONSEQUENCES OF CRIMINAL CONVICTIONS?

MYTH: Any criminal conviction will result in removal, so there is no point in trying to find a safe alternative.

FACT: Your criminal attorney may be able to get you a "safe plea" which will prevent you from suffering any negative immigration consequences, or at least find a plea that will allow you to fight for your right to stay in the U.S. in immigration court. Finding a safe plea might be quite simple. You need to tell your criminal attorney that you are concerned about immigration consequences so you can get proper advice.

MYTH: My criminal attorney does not need to know details about my immigration status or prior criminal history.

FACT: This information can drastically change what pleas would be safe for you to take. DHS has different rules for different types of immigration statuses, such as LPRs vs. refugees. In some cases, a prior conviction can affect whether a plea to a current charge is safe because some removal charges depend on having two or more convictions.

MYTH: If my criminal attorney says I'm fine and that she doesn't need to do any research into my options, I can trust that she is right.

FACT: Law dealing with immigration consequences is extremely complicated and constantly changing. Your criminal attorney may never know that you are not a U.S. citizen unless you tell her. Even if your criminal attorney is aware of your immigration status, she may not have the necessary knowledge of immigration law required to give you the best advice. Don't be afraid to ask your attorney whether she has experience in immigration law. If she does not, ask her to find an immigration lawyer to assist her. Remember that you have a constitutional right to receive this information from your criminal attorney.

MYTH: Only a private attorney will be able to handle these complicated issues.

FACT: The Supreme Court specifically mentions public defenders as attorneys who are *required* to inform clients about potential immigration consequences of any criminal plea. Your public defender should have resources available to assist him. It is your right to have this information and public defenders must provide it. You should *never* agree to a plea if you are uncertain about how it will affect your immigration status.

MYTH: If the state in which I face criminal charges doesn't assign me a public defender or the crime is not a misdemeanor or felony, the conviction isn't serious enough to cause immigration problems for me.

FACT: Many states have a category of criminal convictions known by terms such as "summary offenses," "infractions," or "violations" that are considered less serious than misdemeanors under state law. Depending on the state, you may not be assigned a public defender for these cases. For many *non-immigration purposes,* these dispositions may not count as a conviction, but *they may still affect your immigration status,* and you should talk to an attorney who understands these issues.

WHAT ARE THE IMMIGRATION CONSEQUENCES OF CRIMINAL CONVICTIONS?

What You Need to Know While You are Facing Criminal Charges

MYTH: If I pay a criminal bail, I will be free while my criminal case is pending, no matter what.

FACT: If you are arrested for a criminal charge, the Department of Homeland Security (DHS) may issue a "detainer" against you. If this happens, paying your criminal bond may only result in your being transferred into immigration custody, which could mean being detained hundreds of miles away from your family and from the criminal court handling your case.

Once you are in DHS custody, you may be given an immigration bond. This must be paid in addition to your criminal bond. Unlike criminal bonds, 100% of the amount of the immigration bond must be paid before you can be released. If you are convicted in criminal court, you may lose the ability to get the money paid for your immigration bond back. Many individuals in immigration custody are not even allowed to apply for a bond. If you fall into this category, you could be stuck in DHS custody until your immigration case ends. Any time spent in immigration detention during your criminal proceedings will not count for "time served" or other types of credits that can reduce the overall time you spend incarcerated for a criminal sentence, unlike time in criminal custody. This could mean that you are better off not paying a criminal bond. There is also a possibility that the detainer was issued by mistake, meaning that you may get to leave custody after paying a criminal bond.

CHAPTER 4

Things to Know After Your Criminal Proceedings

MYTH: If I am convicted of a crime and DHS begins removal proceedings against me I am doomed.

FACT: Even if a conviction has immigration consequences and you end up in removal proceedings as a result, there are often forms of relief available, as well as other remedies you may eligible for. Before you give up, talk to an immigration lawyer or legal services provider who can evaluate your case—ideally in cooperation with a criminal defense attorney who understands the immigration consequences of criminal convictions.

MYTH: Once I have a criminal conviction, there is no changing it.

FACT: Depending on your case, you may be able to obtain post-conviction relief (PCR). PCR is a process in which a criminal attorney goes into court and seeks to have your sentence reduced or your conviction changed.

If you pled guilty because your criminal defense attorney instructed you to, but failed to tell you there would be immigration consequences to your guilty plea, you may be able to have your conviction changed, and your removal order reevaluated. For more information, see the Florence Project's guide at www.firrp.org/media/Padilla-v.-Kentucky-Guide-2013.pdf.

MYTH: If my conviction does not have immigration consequences, I do not need to list it on any immigration forms.

FACT: You *must* follow the instructions on all immigration forms.

WHAT ARE THE IMMIGRATION CONSEQUENCES OF CRIMINAL CONVICTIONS?

Those forms usually request that you list *all* contacts with law enforcement, including arrests, citations, and convictions. Not listing a conviction puts you at risk of being accused of fraud. DHS will discover your conviction even if you don't tell them. Your failure to disclose your conviction will be viewed negatively. This could prevent you from obtaining certain immigration benefits, including U.S. citizenship. In most cases, it is much better to list everything and explain it rather than omit it and wait for Immigration to confront you with it.

MYTH: If I get an expungement or pardon of my conviction, it no longer exists for immigration purposes.

FACT: Many states have expungement programs that will remove a conviction from your record for state purposes. However, DHS often does *not* treat these expunged convictions as erased, so you must still disclose them, and they may still affect you. A pardoned conviction may not have immigration consequences but still might need to be disclosed.

MYTH: I can travel outside of the U.S. without worry after a criminal conviction.

FACT: The U.S. uses different legal rules for immigrants entering the country than for immigrants already living here. Even if you leave the country for just a short trip, upon your return, the U.S. will apply the same rules used for immigrants coming to the U.S. for the first time. This means that a conviction that did not cause you problems within the U.S. might get you placed in removal proceedings after a trip abroad. As technology improves, even people with older convictions who have traveled abroad several times sometimes have immigration problems upon returning because it is easier for Immigration to find the information. You should ask your criminal lawyer if a plea will affect your right to travel.

MYTH: If I'm not convicted of a crime in criminal court, I won't have any immigration problems related to that incident.

FACT: In most cases it is true that DHS cannot remove you based on alleged criminal conduct if you weren't convicted. However, there are some exceptions to this rule. The most common relate to drug trafficking and alien smuggling. If you are accused of this type of crime, you may have to defend yourself in immigration court even if you weren't convicted. Unfortunately, while in criminal court charges against you must be proved beyond a reasonable doubt, in immigration court the standard of proof is only "clear and convincing evidence." Thus, evidence that is insufficient to prove your guilt in a criminal court may be enough in immigration court.

CHAPTER 5

What Are Your Rights If You Have Been Arrested?

No matter what your immigration status is, you have certain U.S. constitutional rights including these:

- the right to remain silent
- the right to be free from unfair arrests and searches
- the right to talk to your lawyer if you are arrested

More About Your Rights in a Criminal Matter

The Right to Remain Silent

If the police, ICE, Federal Bureau of Investigation (FBI), or any law enforcement agent approaches you for a criminal matter, you have the right to remain silent. This means that you do not have to answer any questions until you talk to your lawyer. Some states have laws that require you to give them your name or show identity information if you are detained. Check with a lawyer or BIA accredited representative about your state's laws.

Important! Although you have the right to remain silent, **you *do not* have the right to lie to police or immigration officials.** This is a crime, and could result in your deportation and inability to return to the U.S. If you do not want to reveal your immigration status or answer any other questions, it is very important that you do not lie, but instead remain silent, and wait to speak to a lawyer before answering questions.

Be sure to always have with you the phone number of a lawyer's office that you can call. A lawyer can explain how you can best protect your rights. If you don't have the number of an immigration lawyer who will take your call, the following agencies can help you find one:

- AILA (American Immigration Lawyers Association) Immigration Lawyer Referral Service: www.ailalawyer.com, (202-216-2400)
- National Lawyers Guild, National Immigration Project: www.nationalimmigrationproject.org, (617-227-9727)
- Immigration Law Help: www.immigrationlawhelp.org (search by state)
- EOIR Free Legal Service Provider List: www.justice.gov/eoir/probono/states.htm (search by state)

If you have valid immigration papers, you should carry them with you and be prepared to show them to officers. Examples of immigration documents include your I-94, green card, visa, border crossing document, or even court documents showing you are in proceedings if you have no other papers. (See Chapter 7, "Case Status and Proof of Status," for more information on how to show your status.) Make sure you have a copy of your immigration papers in a safe place at home in case your originals are lost or stolen. If you do not have valid immigration papers, you can choose to not answer questions about your status or papers, but you may be arrested.

WHAT ARE YOUR RIGHTS IF YOU HAVE BEEN ARRESTED?

Important! ***Never show false papers, or claim you have U.S. citizenship or another valid immigration status if you do not.*** This is a crime, and may result in your deportation and inability to return to the U.S.

You do not have to answer any other questions if an officer stops you on the street, visits where you work or live, or calls you on the telephone. Instead, you can ask to speak to your lawyer. If you have been stopped for reasons related to criminal activity, you have the right to request a government-appointed lawyer.

The Right to Be Free From "Unreasonable Searches and Seizures"
If the police stop you on the street, an officer can frisk you, which means pat your clothing to see if you are carrying anything illegal. But that is all. If they stop you in your car, they can search without a warrant if they have a good reason to suspect illegal activity.

However, usually to search or enter your house, the police must show you a warrant. If police come to your house, ask to see their warrant. If they do not have one, you do not have to let them in. Even if they have a warrant and enter, you still have the right to remain silent.

Your Rights When Facing ICE Detention and Deportation
A USCIS or ICE official may ask to see your immigration papers. If you have valid immigration papers, it is a good idea to show them to the official. If you do not show them, the official may arrest you. ***Again, do not lie, or present fake papers or papers that belong to someone else.***

CHAPTER 5

Important! You do not have to answer any questions about where you are from, how you got to the U.S., or your immigration status (whether you are undocumented) without talking to a lawyer—even if you are arrested. *Do not* sign anything, especially an "Order of Voluntary Departure" or anything admitting that you used false identification or travel documents, without talking to a lawyer first. If you admit you are undocumented or sign those papers, you could lose rights to stay that you might otherwise have.

If ICE detains you, ICE officials may decide to do one or more of the following:

- Begin the immigration proceedings to remove you from the U.S.
- Activate an old removal order without going through immigration court
- Hold you in custody
- Release you

They usually must make this decision within 48 hours. If they still have not decided after 48 hours in detention, talk to your lawyer. If you have no lawyer, ask ICE for a list of *pro bono* (free) and low-cost lawyers. In immigration proceedings, unlike criminal proceedings, you do not have the right to a government-appointed attorney; however, ICE is required to provide you with a list of immigration legal services providers.

If ICE starts removal proceedings or if you have a final order of removal, ICE may either continue to hold you in custody or release you. If ICE decides to keep you detained, you should ask the Immigration Judge whether you are eligible for a bond hearing. You should also ask an attorney for help with this.

WHAT ARE YOUR RIGHTS IF YOU HAVE BEEN ARRESTED?

You have the right to contact your home country's consulate or the consulate of the country where you have your citizenship. You have the right to refuse to talk to your home country's consulate. It is your choice.

Usually, you have the right to a hearing in front of an Immigration Judge. ICE usually cannot deport you unless you have a hearing. If you accept "voluntary departure," you will not have a hearing. If you accept "voluntary departure" or removal, you have given up your rights and may never be able to enter the U.S. again.

Important! If you are released, it does not mean your case is over. Make sure you understand what the next steps in your case are, and when you next need to be in immigration court. Failure to show up to your court hearings may lead to your deportation and inability to return to the U.S.

Important! Your constitutional rights rarely change, but immigration laws and regulations do change. If you are not sure about your rights or if you fear that your rights may have been violated, call the National Lawyers Guild at 617-227-9727 or the American Civil Liberties Union at 212-549-2660.

What Can I Do If My Rights Were Violated in Detention?
There are a number of steps you can take if your rights were violated while in detention.

ICE Community Hotline
You or your relatives may call the ICE Community Hotline at 1-888-351-4024 to report abuses or other problems with your treatment.

CHAPTER 5

Office for Civil Rights and Civil Liberties

If you experienced any type of abuse; civil rights or human rights violations; or discrimination based on your race, ethnicity, national origin, gender, or a disability; you can file a report with the Office for Civil Rights and Civil Liberties (CRCL). CRCL is a division of the Department of Homeland Security (DHS) that investigates reports of such violations.

Copies of the complaint form are available in detention centers. You can also download a copy at www.dhs.gov/xlibrary/assets/crcl-complaint-submission-form-english.pdf, and read more about the process at www.dhs.gov/file-civil-rights-complaint. Mail, fax, or email the form to:

Office for Civil Rights and Civil Liberties
245 Murray Lane, SW
Building 410, Mail Stop #0800
Washington, DC 20528
Phone: 1-866-644-8360
Fax: 202-401-4708
E-mail: civil.liberties@dhs.gov

You can also call or send a letter or email with a description of what happened to the following two departments, which also conduct investigations into ICE:

DHS Office of Inspector General
Attention: Office of Investigations Hotline
245 Murray Drive SW
Building 410, Mail Stop #2600
Washington, DC 20528
Phone: 1-800-323-8603
E-mail: DHSOIGHOTLINE@dhs.gov

WHAT ARE YOUR RIGHTS IF YOU HAVE BEEN ARRESTED?

ICE Office of Professional Responsibility
Department of Homeland Security
Immigration and Customs Enforcement
Office of Professional Responsibility
P.O. Box 14475
Pennsylvania Avenue NW
Washington, DC 20044
E-mail: Joint.Intake@dhs.gov

Some information in this section courtesy of National Lawyers Guild, ACLU, and Florence Immigrant and Refugee Rights Project.

CHAPTER 6

How to Get Your Personal Property After You Are Released From Detention

This section is for those who have been released from immigration detention.

Check-In Process

When you came to the detention center an officer took your property. The processing officers gave you receipts for your property. They should return your property when they release you. You should have two receipts:

- Form G-589: a white paper describing personal property, including documents and cash (money)
- Form I-77: a ticket for luggage and a description of contents.

Check-Out Process

When you left detention, you and the officer should have checked that you received everything written on the G-589 and I-77 forms. There are three reasons why you might not leave with all your property:

- You gave a shipping address for large luggage. The address where your luggage was sent and the date it was sent should also be written on the appropriate I-77 form.
- ICE reserved the right to appeal the Immigration Judge's decision and is keeping your original documents in your A-file—the folder with your case information.
- Something was lost.

If ICE Appeals

ICE may reserve the right to appeal the judge's decision in your immigration case. ICE must appeal within 30 days. If you have not been notified of an appeal within 30 days, you can get back your documents.

To find out if your case is being appealed, call the USCIS information hotline at 1-800-375-5283, or check the status of your case online at https://egov.uscis.gov/cris/Dashboard/CaseStatus.do.

To get back your documents, call the detention center and ask for help. If you remember the name of your deportation officer, ask for him or her directly. If you do not remember the officer's name, ask for the processing unit.

If ICE Sent Your Documents Somewhere Else

If your deportation officer sent the documents to another ICE office, it may be more difficult to find them again. But it is still your right to have your property returned to you. Ask your deportation officer to give you the address of the ICE office where your documents were sent.

Call USCIS at 1-800-870-3676 and ask for form G-884 or go online to replace with www.uscis.gov/g-884. This form is a request to get back your original documents. Photocopy your completed G-884 form and keep the copy for your records. Send the completed original form by mail with a return receipt, available at the post office, to the ICE office that holds the documents you want back. Keep the receipt in a safe place with a copy of the form. Call the USCIS National Customer Service Center at 1-800-375-5283 if you do not know the address of the ICE office that holds your documents.

Note on Identification Documents (IDs)

ICE attorneys unfortunately often will not return your passport or other forms of identification until after your case is over. This is because they want to use your identification as evidence in your immigration court case. This can make it difficult for you to access basic services you may want, like public benefits, or to drive if ICE has kept your driver's license. Sometimes, your lawyer will be able to convince ICE to agree to make copies of your documents for their records and give you the originals. Ask your lawyer for help with this.

Get a Copy of Your Medical Record

If you saw the detention center's doctor for any health problems while you were in detention, you should ask for a copy of your medical record. If you were receiving medical care when you were released from the detention center, they should have given you a discharge plan to ensure continuity of medical care. This discharge plan is a written copy of your medical records and what you will need to do to still receive care after you are released. If you were getting prescription medications at the time of your release, they may have given you up to a 30-day supply of the medication.

If you do not have your medical record, call the detention center and ask how to get a copy. Ask them to send the copy to you, to your Resettlement Agency if you have one, or to your lawyer. You must sign a Freedom of Information Act (FOIA) form to let the detention center send a copy to the Resettlement Agency. This form is used when asking for your confidential records from a government office.

If you need help locating the detention center in which you were held, call the USCIS National Customer Service Center at 1-800-375-5283.

If you do not get a response from ICE, contact an immigration lawyer or BIA accredited representative.

CHAPTER 7

Case Status and Proof of Status

If you have been granted some form of legal protective status to stay in the U.S., you should have a document that shows your immigration status. This U.S. government document is your "proof of status" and will be important when you apply for immigration benefits. These documents can also be used as forms of identification to apply for the various benefits described in this guide.

If you do not know the status of your immigration case with USCIS, check the status of your case at https://egov.uscis.gov/cris/Dashboard/CaseStatus.do. You can also call the USCIS National Customer Service Center at 1-800-375-5283. You will likely be asked for your name, date of birth, A-number, and a receipt number for your pending application. If you have questions about your case, you can make a free Infopass appointment to speak with a USCIS representative at https://infopass.uscis.gov/.

If you have a case in Immigration Court, and wish to check the date of your next hearing, case status, or other information, call the Executive Office for Immigration Review's Case Information System at 240-314-1500 or 1-800-898-7180. You will need your A-number.

Following is a list of documents that prove your status, organized by status:

Refugees

The following documents prove your immigration status as a refugee:

- ***I-94 Identification Card:*** Also known as an "Arrival and Departure Record," this was given to upon your arrival to the U.S. by Immigration officials. It is usually a white card with a stamp that states your status, A-number, name, and country of origin. In May 2013, many I-94s became automated, so instead of receiving an actual card, you may have received an annotated I-94 stamp affixed to your passport. This stamp is the same thing as the old I-94 card, and can be used as ID as well.
- ***Employment Authorization Document (EAD):*** As a refugee, you should be issued your EAD, or work permit, soon after you arrive in the U.S. It should have the code (a)(3), which is the code for "refugee."

The following documents support, but do not prove, your immigration status as a refugee:

- The resettlement documents you received from the International Organization for Migration (IOM), in your IOM bag, before you departed your home country
- Your promissory note from your travel loan
- Medical exam forms from your refugee medical exam (it is highly recommended that you not share these forms, however)
- IOM card given to you at the port of entry (the U.S. airport

where you arrived) that contains your basic information and emergency contact information.

Asylees

The following documents prove your immigration status as an asylee:

- ***I-94 Identification Card:*** Also known as an "Arrival and Departure Record," this was given to you when you were granted aslyee status. It is usually a white card with a stamp that states your status, A-number, name, and country of origin. In May 2013, many I-94s became automated, so instead of receiving an actual card, you may have received an annotated I-94 stamp affixed to your passport. This stamp is the same thing as the old I-94 card, and can be used as ID as well.
- ***Immigration Judge Court Order:*** This is the document you received if you were granted asylum in Immigration Court by a judge. If the judge's order says that USCIS "reserves its right to appeal," you will have to wait 31 days to know if you were given protective status. On or after the 31st day, you can call the USCIS hotline number or go to the website where you check your status to see if your case was appealed. If it was not appealed, you have protective status. If you have a judge's order but not an I-94 card, you should go to your local USCIS office and ask how to get an I-94 card.
- ***Asylum Office Grant Letter:*** This is the letter you received from USCIS if you were granted asylum by an Asylum Officer, and not in immigration court. This letter should have an I-94 attached at the bottom. If it does not, contact the USCIS office where you had your interview.
- ***Employment Authorization Document (EAD):*** As an aslyee, you do not need an EAD, or work permit, to work. You may

choose to get one for convenience. It should have the code (a)(5), which is code for "asylee."

A family member who receives asylum through you may prove his or her status with an I-730 Approval Letter.

Asylum Seekers

You will receive a receipt after filing a petition for asylum status, which serves as proof of your application for asylum while your case is reviewed.

If you file your petition in court you unfortunately will not receive a receipt, and it is harder to prove your status as an asylum seeker. If you need to prove your status to immigration officials, you can use your A-number or any court documents or orders from Immigration Judges, including your Notice to Appear (NTA), which is the document explaining why you are being called to court for removal proceedings.

Some asylum seekers will also be able to get an EAD, or work permit, which is covered in Chapter 14, "Right to Work," and Chapter 15, "How to Get a Work Permit." If you get a work permit, your permit will have the code (c)(8) for "Asylum Applicant," and you should use this as ID. You may also be eligible for a limited Social Security number, which is discussed in Chapter 16, "How to Get a Social Security Number." If so, you will receive a Social Security card, although this will not have your photo on it. Some asylum seekers will be able to get a state ID card, which is briefly discussed in Chapter 17, "How to Get a State ID Card."

Note: Sometimes you will not be allowed to enter a government building without a photo ID, which can make it difficult to apply for certain benefits. You may want to try to get a state ID to avoid this difficulty.

Withholding of Removal, Under the INA or Under CAT (Convention Against Torture)

Unfortunately, there is no official way for you to prove your status. Like asylum seekers, your A-number, NTA, or the order from the Immigration Judge found on the court document you received after your court hearing may be the only documents that show proof of your status.

Some people granted withholding or CAT protection may be eligible for an EAD, or work permit, which is covered in Chapter 14, "Right to Work," and Chapter 15, "How to Get a Work Permit." If you get a work permit, your permit will have the code (a)(10) for "Withholding of Removal," and you should use this as ID. You may also be eligible for a limited Social Security number, which is discussed in Chapter 16, "How to Get a Social Security Number." If so, you will receive a Social Security card, although this will not have your photo on it. Some states may permit you to get a state ID card or driver's license, which is discussed in Chapter 17, "How to Get a State ID Card."

Deferral Under CAT (Convention Against Torture)

Unfortunately, there is no official way for you to prove your status. Like asylum seekers, your A-number, NTA, or the order from the Immigration Judge found on the court document you received after your court hearing may be the only documents that show your status. It is rare, but some people granted deferral under CAT protection may be eligible for a work permit, which is covered in Chapter 14, "Right to Work," and Chapter 15, "How to Get a Work Permit." If you get a work permit, it will have the code (c)(18), the code for "final order of removal but cannot be removed." You may also be eligible for a limited Social Security number, which is discussed in Chapter 16, "How to Get a Social Security Number." If so, you will receive a Social Security card, although this will not have your photo on it. Some states may permit you to get a state ID card or driver's license, which is briefly discussed in Chapter 17, "How to Get a State ID Card."

Tip: Your proof of status is a very important document. Keep your proof of status protected in a safe and dry place to prevent it from getting torn or destroyed. You may want to keep it in a lock box or a bank safe. Make a photocopy to keep with you until you get a work permit or state ID card.

Can I Lose My Legal Protective Status?

Until you become a U.S. citizen, you can lose your protective status under certain circumstances. Your protective status with a T-visa and U-visa will expire if you do not get a green card and can be cancelled if you do not comply with the rules of the visa. The law says that refugee, parolee, asylum status, WOR, and protection under the CAT are indefinite. **Indefinite does not mean permanent. Indefinite means your protective status will not end on a set date.** The U.S. government may start a process to end your protective status for these reasons:

- Things have changed in the country you fled, and you no longer have a well-founded fear of persecution
- Another country grants you legal protective status
- You commit certain crimes

CHAPTER 8

What You Must Do When You Change Your Address

Notifying USCIS about your change of address is very important! If your case is still pending, it is also very important to notify the immigration court!

The immigration court and USCIS are not the same. If your court case is not finished, or you were given a conditional grant of asylum by the Board of Immigration Appeals, **you must tell the immigration court or BIA your new address within five days after you move.** If your case is in Immigration Court, you can get the change of address form, EOIR-33, from the immigration court or online at www.justice.gov/eoir/eoirforms/eoir33/ICadr33.htm, and then follow the directions to download the proper form according to the location of your court. If your case is at the BIA, use this form: www.justice.gov/eoir/eoirforms/eoir33bia.pdf. You may also need to change your case to a new court. For more information on how to change the venue (location of court), talk to an immigration attorney or BIA accredited representative, or go online to the EOIR's website at www.usdoj.gov/eoir.

CHAPTER 8

If you won your immigration case and the government did not appeal after one month, then your court case is finished and you do not have to tell the immigration court or BIA your new address.

However, USCIS will still need to send you important documents. All non-citizens must tell USCIS when they move—even if you won your immigration case. **You must tell USCIS your new address within 10 days after you move.** To avoid trouble, you should tell USCIS before you move, and give USCIS the date that your new address becomes effective.

If you do not tell USCIS when you move, one of these things may happen:

- You may have to pay a large fine.
- You may have to go to prison for 30 days.
- You may be deported.

How to Notify USCIS About Your Change of Address

To tell USCIS when you move, fill out form AR-11, the Alien's Change of Address Card. This can be done in one of three ways:

- Go to https://egov.uscis.gov/coa/displayCOAForm.do to fill out and submit the form online.
- Call the USCIS National Customer Service Center at 1-800-375-5283 and follow the instructions for an address change.
- Request the most recent version of form AR-11, the Alien's Change of Address Card, by calling USCIS at 1-800-870-3676 or retrieving it online at http://www.uscis.gov/addresschange. Fill it out and send it to the following address:

WHAT YOU MUST DO
WHEN YOU CHANGE YOUR ADDRESS

U.S. Department of Homeland Security
Citizenship and Immigration Services
Attn: Change of Address
1344 Pleasants Drive
Harrisonburg, VA 22801

Remember these things:

- If you have pending or recently approved applications, and you submit your Change of Address form on paper (by mail), you must also change your address for each pending application by calling 1-800-375-5283. If you submit your Change of Address form online, you do not have to take this extra step, so you may want to submit it online because it is easier and covers all your applications.
- All forms must be completed in English.
- If you call to get the AR-11 form, you may want to request it as soon as you know you are going to move, since it may take more than 10 days to arrive.
- Keep a photocopy of the completed form for your records. Send the form via certified mail with a return receipt, available at the post office. Keep the proof of mailing, and put that and the photocopy of the completed form together in a safe place.
- To be on the safe side, send a copy to each USCIS Service Center where you have sent immigration paperwork or applications.

USCIS may request the filing date and a copy of the cover page for any applications you have pending with a service center (an

EAD or I-730, for example). To confirm where to send the AR-11 form or to learn what else you should submit, call the USCIS National Customer Service Center at 1-800-375-5283 or see www.uscis.gov/addresschange.

Other Places to Notify About Your Change of Address

You may move a few times while you are getting settled in the U.S. It is important that you maintain a reliable postal address. You must inform any social services and Refugee Agencies you have been working with when you move, as well as any local, state, or federal government agency with which you have pending business. You should also notify banks, credit card companies, doctors, and other places with which you have business, that send you bills or mail, or that otherwise need to contact you.

If you move, go to the post office and tell them you have changed your address. They will give you a paper to fill out with your name, your old address and your new address. You can ask them to forward your mail for up to six months. This means they can make sure that letters that were sent to your old address will go instead to your new home. No government documents will be forwarded so make sure to communicate your current address to the government.

CHAPTER 9

How to Reunite Your Family

For many people who have fled their home to seek protection, leaving their families behind is the most painful part of the journey.

A family reunification process allows some immigrants to bring their family members. If you have refugee or asylee status, you can petition to bring your spouse and unmarried children under 21, in a process outlined below. This section also outlines how asylum seekers can add family members to their asylum applications. Once you become a lawful permanent resident, you can apply to bring unmarried children of any age, and once you become a U.S. citizen, you can apply to bring even more categories of family members by filling out the Form I-130. Following are status-specific details.

Refugees and Asylees

If you have been in the U.S. for less than two years as a refugee or were granted asylum within the past two years, you can apply for your spouse (husband or wife) and any unmarried children under the age of 21 to join you here. It is very important that you apply for visas for your spouse and children **within two years** of the time you were granted asylum or entered the U.S. as a refugee. If you wait more than two years, you will no longer be able to use the special family reunification process, and will have to wait many years before they can join you.

Fill out an I-730, Refugee/Asylee Relative Petition, found at www.uscis.gov/i-730. You must fill out a separate I-730 for each family member you wish to bring. There is no fee for the application, but you will need to pay for a plane ticket for each person. Do not buy plane tickets for your family members until you receive authorization for them to come to the U.S. Once granted, your family members will usually have to use the visa to come to the U.S. within a few months. You may be able to get a loan from a church or another organization to pay for their plane ticket, but this is rare.

You should get help from a BIA accredited organization or immigration lawyer to help you file this form. Be sure to carefully read all the instructions. Here are a few things to keep in mind:

- You will need proof that the people you want to bring to the U.S. are your relatives. Photographs, birth certificates, and marriage certificates will help you prove this.
- You will have to pay for the airplane tickets for your family members to join you. Start saving money!
- Make sure you include copies of all necessary supporting documents mentioned in the form's instructions. USCIS may delay or deny your application if these supporting documents are not included.
- After you file your immigration form, USCIS may write a letter telling you that your relative will need to have a

biometrics appointment. This means they will take your relative's fingerprints. They may also ask for a signature and take a picture. USCIS will give you details on where your relative must go for their biometrics appointment. Sometimes, a DNA test may be required for you and for the relative you are applying to bring. You may have to pay for these tests.

- Keep a photocopy of the completed form for your records. Send the form via certified mail with a return receipt, available at the post office.

Priority 3 (P-3) Family Reunification Program

There is another process you may be able to use called the Priority-3 (P-3) Family Reunification Program, or Affidavit of Relationship program. This process is only for people of certain nationalities that the U.S. government decides each year, based on the level of danger in each country. These applications are done by refugee resettlement offices, which must fill them out free of charge. If your family is accepted through this program, they will be brought into the country as refugees. Check with a Resettlement Agency, listed in Chapter 25, on whether the P-3 program applies to you.

Asylum Seekers

Unfortunately, you cannot bring your family to the U.S. while you wait for your asylum claim to be decided. However, you must list your spouse and children on your I-589, Application for Asylum and for Withholding of Removal, when you apply for asylum. If your spouse and unmarried children under 21 are already in the U.S., you can add them, and they will be included in your application. If your spouse and unmarried children under 21 are not in the U.S., you may apply to bring them if you are granted asylum, within two years of receiving asylum. You can apply by filling out an I-730,

Refugee/Asylee Relative Petition, found at www.uscis.gov/i-730. Follow the instructions under the section above for refugees and asylees.

Withholding of Removal and CAT

Unfortunately, you cannot bring your family members to the U.S.

CHAPTER 10

How to Get Your Green Card

What is Lawful Permanent Residence?

The term "lawful permanent resident," also known as "LPR," has the same meaning as "legal permanent resident," "permanent resident alien," and "green card holder." If you are an LPR, the U.S. government allows you to live permanently in the U.S. as long as you do not commit particular crimes or otherwise violate the terms of your status. You can work anywhere in the U.S. (except for certain jobs that require U.S. citizenship), travel in and out of the country with some restrictions, and have protection under all U.S. laws.

As an LPR, you are required to obey all laws of the U.S., file income taxes, report income to the federal and state government, and if you are a male between the ages of 18 and 25, register with the Selective Service. You are not allowed to vote in federal elections. Although a few states and communities allow you to vote, it is very uncommon. Failure to abide by the above requirements can threaten your immigration status and make you subject to deportation.

CHAPTER 10

The process of gaining lawful permanent residence is also called "adjustment of status," or "AOS." Green cards used to be printed on green paper, but no longer are.

Being an LPR is a necessary first step before becoming a citizen of the U.S. You can apply for U.S. citizenship after meeting certain conditions for five years as an LPR. Information for people who have LPR status is covered more in-depth on the supplement for LPRs. This document can be found at: www.lirs.org/firststeps.

Who is Eligible to Become a Lawful Permanent Resident?

To be an LPR, you first must figure out whether you are eligible. For detailed information, see www.uscis.gov/green-card/green-card-processes-and-procedures/green-card-eligibility. The eligibility requirements are very strict. There are four general categories of eligibility:

1. Family sponsorship
2. Employment sponsorship
3. Adjustment from refugee or asylee status
4. Other special provisions

Family Sponsorship: Some people may be able to adjust through their U.S. citizen or LPR family member. There are many categories within the family sponsorship track, which have different processes and wait times.

- Immediate relatives: These relatives of U.S. citizens do not have to wait for a visa to become available, and there is no limitation on the number available each year:
  - Parents of a U.S. citizen who is at least 21,
  - Spouse (husband or wife) of a U.S. citizen,

  - o Unmarried children under 21 of a U.S. citizen.
- Qualified relatives: These relatives of U.S. citizens or LPRs will have to wait for a visa to become available before they can apply, and the wait time depends on the preference category (shortest wait time for the 1st preference, and longest for the 4th):
  - o First Preference: Unmarried, adult (21 or older) sons and daughters of U.S. citizens
  - o Second Preference A: Spouses and unmarried children (under 21) of LPRs
  - o Second Preference B: Unmarried sons and daughters (21 or older) of LPRs
  - o Third Preference: Married sons and daughters of U.S. citizens, their spouses, and their minor children
  - o Fourth Preference: Siblings (brothers and sisters) of adult U.S. citizens, their spouses, and their minor children

If you think you might be eligible to adjust through a family member, see a lawyer or BIA accredited representative. Also see USCIS's page on adjustment through family members at www.uscis.gov/green-card/green-card-through-family.

Employment Sponsorship: Some people become eligible to adjust through employment in various ways, including an offer of permanent employment; substantial investment in an enterprise that creates new jobs in the U.S.; extraordinary ability or national interest waiver; or another special employment category such as religious workers, translators, or medical professionals from specific countries. For more information, see USCIS's page on employment sponsorship at www.uscis.gov/green-card/green-card-through-job.

Adjustment from Refugee or Asylee status: Refugees must apply to adjust one year after admission to the U.S. as a refugee, and asylees are eligible to adjust one year after they are granted aslyee status. The process for refugees and aslyees is outlined in detail below.

Other Special Provisions: You may also be eligible to adjust through other special provisions. These include the Diversity Visa Immigrant Program (green card lottery), Cuban/Haitian entrants, fiancées of U.S. citizens and their children, and other programs. For more information on these specific categories, please see USCIS's page on other ways to get a green card at www.uscis.gov/green-card/other-ways-get-green-card.

This category also includes the ability to adjust through other humanitarian protection-based categories, such as through VAWA for battered spouses, children, or parents; a T-visa for trafficking victims; and a U-visa for immigrant victims of crime. Among other requirements, battered spouses, children, or parents are eligible to adjust as soon as their I-360 for VAWA protection is approved; trafficking victims are eligible three years after being granted a T-visa; and crime victims are eligible three years after being granted a U-visa. Detailed instructions on how to adjust from those special humanitarian-based categories will appear in the supplements for those specific statuses.

How to Become a Lawful Permanent Resident

The steps to becoming an LPR vary by status and which options are available to you. Specific instructions are available for each status, either below for refugees and asylees, or in status-specific supplements. Regardless of status, everyone must fill out an I-485, Application to Register Permanent Residence or Adjust Status. You can request the most recent version of form I-485 by calling USCIS at 1-800-870-3676 or you can get the form online at www.uscis.gov/i-485. If you can, get help from a BIA accredited representative or a lawyer.

Note on Maintaining, Renewing, and Replacing Your Green Card
Most green cards are valid for 10 years, and you must renew your green card before it expires. (Those with "conditional permanent residence" must take steps to remove the condition and renew after two years.) You also must replace your green card if it is lost, stolen, damaged, or if your name or other biographical information changes.

Once you get your green card, you must remember that it can still be taken away if you commit certain crimes, fail to pay taxes, or stay out of the U.S. for a lengthy period of time.

For more information on how to renew or replace your green card, and how to make sure you do not lose your LPR status, see the supplement on lawful permanent residents.

Refugees

As a refugee, you are **required** to apply to adjust your status one year after being admitted to the U.S. as a refugee. Note: When permanent residency is granted, you will have your adjustment of status date recorded as the *day you entered into the U.S. as a refugee,* not the date you actually adjusted. This is helpful because in order to become a U.S. citizen, you must have been an LPR for five years (among other requirements). As a refugee, your first year in the U.S. will count towards that five-year requirement if you file your green card application on time. In other words, refugees and asylees may apply to naturalize after having a green card for four years, instead of five.

CHAPTER 10

You should submit the following forms and information:

- Form I-485, Application to Register Permanent Residence or Adjust Status.
- Two passport-sized photos in an envelope stapled to lower left corner. (Be sure the staple does not go through the photo, and that your name and A-number are written on the back of the photo but that the ink did not go through, or the application will be rejected!)
- Form G-28, if applicable, signed by you and the attorney (or authorized representative).
- Form G-325A, the Biographical Information Form.
- Form I-693, Report of Medical Examination and Vaccination Record.
    - Note: you only need the complete Form I-693 if you had "medical grounds of inadmissibility" when you arrived, or if you received refugee status through a relative. Otherwise, you only need the vaccination portion filled out. Call the National Customer Service Center at 1-800-375-5283 or see the Civil Surgeons Locator page on the USCIS website at www.uscis.gov/civilsurgeons to locate USCIS-designated civil surgeons (doctors) where you live.
- Evidence of your refugee status (see Chapter 7, "Case Status and Proof of Status").
- Proof of any legal name change you obtained since gaining refugee status. If you have married or divorced, include copies of the marriage documents, and proof of your current and former name.

You must prepare a separate Form I-485 application packet for each member of your family who wishes to obtain a green card.

HOW TO GET YOUR GREEN CARD

All family members' application packets should be mailed together in the same mailing envelope. To hold each application packet together, use a single staple or a paper clip.

Where you send your application depends on the state you live in. Read the instructions on the I-485 page or call the USCIS National Customer Service Center at 1-800-375-5283 and ask where to send the I-485 form.

Asylees

Although it is not required, it is highly recommended that you apply to adjust your status as soon as one year has passed since you were granted asylum.

You should submit the following forms and information:

- Form I-485, Application to Register Permanent Residence or Adjust Status.
- Fee: Unlike refugees, asylees must pay the I-485 fee and the fingerprint fee. It is expensive, so start saving!
    - Note: If you cannot afford the fee, you may be eligible for a "fee waiver," which means you may not have to pay. You should not let the high cost discourage you from applying. Instead, check out USCIS's information on fee waivers at www.uscis.gov/feewaiver. Read the instructions, which explain who is eligible, at www.uscis.gov/sites/default/files/files/form/i-912instr.pdf. If you are eligible, fill out Form I-912, Request for Fee Waiver, at www.uscis.gov/sites/default/files/files/form/i-912.pdf.
- Two photos in an envelope stapled to lower left corner. (Be

sure the staple does not go through the photo, and that your name and A-number are written on the back of the photo but that the ink did not go through, or the application will be rejected!)

- Form G-28, if applicable, signed by you and the attorney (or authorized representative).
- Form G-325A, the Biographical Information Form.
- Form I-693, Report of Medical Examination and Vaccination Record.
    - Note: You can call the National Customer Service Center at 1-800-375-5283 or see the Civil Surgeons Locator page on the USCIS website at www.uscis.gov/civilsurgeons to locate USCIS-designated civil surgeons (doctors) where you live.
- Evidence of your asylee status (see Chapter 7, "Case Status and Proof of Status").
- Proof of any legal name change you obtained since gaining refugee status. If you have married or divorced, include copies of the marriage documents, and proof of your current and former name.

Refugees and Asylees

Be sure to carefully read the detailed instructions and remember these things:

- Did you leave the country during the first year after you got refugee or asylee status? If so, those days do not count as part of your 365 total days. For example, if you left the country for 10 days, you cannot apply for a green card until 375 days after you were granted refugee or asylee status.
- Keep a photocopy of the completed form for your records.

Send the form via certified mail with a return receipt, available at the post office.

- If you have a criminal record, you must submit copies of all court documents, as well as a completed Form I-602, Application by Refugee for Waiver of Grounds of Excludability (if applicable). It is **highly recommended** that you see an attorney to apply if you have criminal convictions. Otherwise you may find yourself in removal proceedings!

Where you send your I-485 depends on the state you live in. Go to www.uscis.gov/i-485 or call the USCIS National Customer Service Center at 1-800-375-5283 and ask where to send the I-485 form.

Asylum Seekers

You cannot apply for a green card until one year from the date you are granted asylum.

Withholding of Removal and CAT

Under current law, you cannot apply for a green card or become a lawful permanent resident.

CHAPTER 11

How to Become a U.S. Citizen

What is Naturalization?

Naturalization is the process by which certain non-U.S. citizens can apply to become U.S. citizens. To "naturalize" means to take the required steps to becoming a U.S. citizen.

What Are the Benefits of Naturalizing?

When you naturalize, you will become a U.S. citizen, and have almost all the same rights and protections as U.S. born citizens. U.S. citizens have more rights than lawful permanent residents (LPRs). There are many things only U.S. citizens can do in America, some of which may be very important to you. It is very important for you try to naturalize when you are eligible, so you may receive these rights and protections. As a naturalized U.S. citizen, you will be able to:

- **Keep your lawful status in the United States and no longer be in danger of deportation.**
  This is very important! Even if you have adjusted your status to become an LPR (have your green card) you can still have

your green card taken away and be deported for committing certain crimes, traveling outside the U.S. for too long, or failing to file your income taxes. When you are an American citizen, you cannot be deported.

- **Bring family members to the U.S.**
  U.S. citizens can bring more family members to the U.S. than refugee, asylees, and LPRs. For example, as a refugee or asylee, you can apply for your spouse (husband or wife) and any unmarried children under the age of 21 to join you. As an LPR, you may apply to bring your spouse or unmarried children of any age. But as a U.S. citizen, you may apply to bring your spouse, and children of any age, whether they are unmarried or married. And as a U.S. citizen, you may also apply to bring your parents and siblings (brother and sisters) once you are over 21 years old.
- **Get more government benefits.**
  Immigrants have many restrictions on access to government benefits and healthcare. (See Chapters 18 and 19 for details on immigrants' access to benefits and healthcare.) However, after you naturalize, you will no longer be subject to immigration-related restrictions, and will have access to benefits and healthcare according to the same rules as U.S. citizens.
- **Vote.**
  Only U.S. citizens can vote in federal elections. Many states also only allow U.S. citizens to vote in state elections. Voting to elect officials like the President and members of Congress is an important political right to many U.S. citizens.
- **Serve on a jury.**
  Only U.S. citizens can serve on a federal jury, and many states also only allow U.S. citizens to serve on a jury. Juries help judges make decisions in court cases.

HOW TO BECOME A U.S. CITIZEN

- **Travel abroad with a U.S. passport.**
  You will be able to travel abroad without restrictions on how long you can stay outside the U.S. You will also be able to get help from the U.S. government when you are abroad if you need it.
- **Get U.S. citizenship for children under 18 years of age.**
  Generally, a child born abroad to a U.S. citizen automatically becomes a U.S. citizen. Any children you previously had who were born abroad and were under 18 at the time you become a citizen may also be eligible to become a U.S. citizen. See a lawyer for help with either of these situations. (Children born inside the U.S. are automatically U.S. citizens.)
- **Apply for more federal jobs.**
  Some federal jobs require U.S. citizenship.
- **Become an elected government official.**
  Only U.S. citizens can run in federal elections for the U.S. Senate or House of Representatives, and most state and local governments have similar rules for state and local government positions. Unfortunately, only those born in the U.S. can run for President.
- **Become eligible for more federal grants and scholarships.**
  Many financial aid grants, including college scholarships, are available only to U.S. citizens.

Note: Before you decide to apply to naturalize, you should first determine if you might already be a U.S. citizen. If you were born in the U.S. or a U.S. territory, or if at least one of your parents is a U.S. citizen, you may already be a U.S. citizen. If either of these situations apply to you, see an immigration lawyer immediately to find out whether you may already be a citizen.

CHAPTER 11

Am I Eligible to Become A U.S. Citizen?

You must meet **all** of the following criteria to apply for naturalization:

- Be at least 18 years old, AND
- Have been admitted as lawful permanent resident (LPR) for at least five years (with some exceptions, explained below), AND
- Have "continuous residence" (explained below) in the U.S. for at least five years after receiving your LPR status (green card), AND
- Have been physically present in the U.S. for at least 30 months of the five-year period before applying for naturalization, AND
- Have lived in the state in which you plan to apply for at least three months before applying, AND
- Live in the U.S. continuously from the time of application for naturalization to the time of admission as a U.S. citizen, AND
- Have good moral character (explained below), AND
- Can demonstrate knowledge of civics and English, and pledge allegiance to the Constitution.

Five Years of Lawful Permanent Residence

Typically, naturalization requires five years of status as a green card, or lawful permanent resident. There are however some exceptions:

- Refugees and asylees who adjusted their status and got their green card (LPR status) after one year may count that one year as part of the five. In other words, refugees and asylees may apply to naturalize after having a green card for four years, instead of five.
- If you are applying to naturalize based on your marriage to a U.S. citizen, you may apply after having your green card for three years, instead of five.

- If you have qualifying experience as a U.S. military member, you may be eligible to apply earlier. See USCIS's page on Citizenship for Military Members at www.uscis.gov/military/citizenship-military-personnel-family-members/citizenship-military-members and ask a lawyer.

Continuous Residence

"Continuous residence" means that you have lived in the U.S., and maintained the U.S. as your place of residence (and no other country) on a continuous basis for five years. You can travel and still maintain continuous residence, but there are important restrictions:

- Traveling outside the U.S. and staying outside for a period of six to twelve months in a row may interrupt this period of "continuous residence," meaning you may have to start over.
- Traveling outside the U.S. for a continuous period of one year or longer will most likely interrupt your period of "continuous residence," and you will have to start over.

It is highly recommended that if you travel outside the U.S., you stay abroad for less than six months; otherwise you could lose your period of continuous residence and have to start your five-year waiting period over. There are a few exceptions if you stayed out between six months and one year, but you should see a lawyer for help if that is the case.

"Continuous residence" also means you must file and pay your taxes every year as a lawful permanent resident (LPR). You may not claim "nonresident alien status" on your tax forms to avoid paying your taxes, or you will lose your continuous residence.

CHAPTER 11

Good Moral Character

To become a U.S. citizen, you must demonstrate that you have "good moral character." Generally, this means someone who is honest, pays their taxes, does not commit crimes, and pays their debts.

If you have committed certain crimes, you will never be able to establish good moral character, and will never be able to apply for citizenship. These crimes include murder and any "aggravated felony" of which you were convicted after November 29, 1990. Other crimes may temporarily prevent you from proving you have good moral character and applying for citizenship, but after a period of time, you will be able to apply. If you have been arrested or convicted of any crimes, and wish to naturalize, it is important to see a lawyer to help you determine whether your crimes will permanently or temporarily prevent you from showing good moral character and naturalizing.

Some examples of crimes that might prevent you from showing good moral character include any crime committed with intent to harm someone, using or selling drugs, being married to more than one person at a time, failing to pay court-ordered child support or alimony payments, and lying to gain immigration benefits, among others.

How Do I Become A U.S. Citizen?

To apply for U.S. citizenship, you must first determine whether you are eligible according to the above criteria. You also can work through USCIS's Naturalization Worksheet, which outlines the rules above and helps you determine if you are eligible. Google search "USCIS Naturalization Worksheet" or follow this link:

www.uscis.gov/sites/default/files/USCIS/Resources/Citizenship%20%26%20Naturalization%20Based%20Resources/A%20Guide%20to%20Naturalization/PDFs/M-480.pdf

HOW TO BECOME A U.S. CITIZEN

File Form N-400, Application for Naturalization

If you are eligible, you must file Form N-400, Application for Naturalization. Visit USCIS's page on the N-400 at www.uscis.gov/n-400. Before you fill out the N-400, you should

- Read USCIS's Guide to Naturalization (available at www.uscis.gov/sites/default/files/files/article/M-476.pdf), or get your lawyer or someone at a BIA accredited organization to help you read through and understand it, because the N-400 application makes many references to this document.
- Then, read the N-400 instructions at www.uscis.gov/sites/default/files/files/form/n-400instr.pdf.

Download the N-400, Application for Naturalization at www.uscis.gov/sites/default/files/files/form/n-400.pdf.

Fill out your N-400 carefully, in blue or black ink. It is highly recommended that you get a lawyer or BIA accredited representative to help you. Be sure to put your A-number at the top right-hand corner of each page. Check your information for accuracy, and sign it. Before you file, make sure you have all the required documentation!

Note: Your N-400 asks questions about crimes. It is very important that you answer honestly and report all crimes, even ones you may have gotten expunged (removed) from your record. If you do not tell USCIS about these crimes, they will find out, and may deny your application, even if the crime you failed to report was not a crime that would have caused your application to be denied!

What Do I Include with My Application?

You must submit the following with your application:

- Two identical 2x2 passport-style photos taken within 30 days of filing. Write your name and A-number lightly on the back.
- A copy of your green card.
- The filing fee ($595) and the fee for your biometrics (fingerprinting) appointment ($85).
- Form N-648, Medical Certification for Disability Exceptions **only if you are seeking a medical or age-related exception to the English or civics test requirements** (see below). You can find Form N-648 at www.uscis.gov/n-648.

Where Do I Mail My Application?

Where you should mail your application depends on where you live, so check USCIS's instructions on where to mail your application at www.uscis.gov/n-400. Be sure to make copies and ask for a certified mail receipt!

When Can I File My Application?

You may file your application up to 90 days before you have met the eligibility requirements above, so generally 90 days before you've had continuous residence as an LPR in the U.S. for five years (or for a refugee, four years) and met the other specific requirements.

What Must I Do After I File My Application?

There are still several steps you must take after you submit your application.

Biometrics Appointment

After USCIS receives your application, USCIS will contact you to let you know when you should go to your local USCIS Application Support Center (ASC) for your biometrics (fingerprinting) appointment. USCIS will take your fingerprints and conduct a criminal background check.

Naturalization Interview

USCIS will schedule an interview for you. Be sure to attend this interview on time, and let USCIS know immediately if you have to reschedule. You must bring the following to your naturalization interview:

- A copy of your green card (LPR card)
- A valid state ID (a form of identification, like a driver's license, issued by your state)
- Your passport and any travel documents
- Other relevant documents: Depending on your situation, you may have other documents you should bring. For example, if you were arrested or convicted of a crime, you must bring arrest or court documents. If you had to serve probation, you should bring proof that you completed your probation. For more information on other documents you may want to bring, see USCIS's Guide to Naturalization at www.uscis.gov/sites/default/files/files/article/M-476.pdf.

Several things will happen at your naturalization interview.

1. Interview: USCIS will ask you questions about what you wrote on your N-400. You should bring a copy so you can look at it.
2. Civics and English Tests: You will take two tests, an English test and a civics test. You should dedicate a lot of time to studying before the test. You can access study materials for both tests at www.uscis.gov/citizenship/learners/study-test. Many local community groups that help immigrants offer classes to help you prepare. You can find classes and resources at www.uscis.gov/citizenship/learners/find-help-your-community. If you fail, you will be able to retake it only once. If you fail twice, your application will be denied.

a. The English test will consist of three parts: a test on your speaking ability, reading ability, and writing ability. You can access information on the test, study materials, and practice tests at www.uscis.gov/citizenship/learners/study-test/study-materials-english-test.

b. The civics test will test your knowledge of American history and government. There are 100 questions, and the USCIS officer will pick 10 to ask you. You must get 6 questions correct to pass. You may find the questions at www.uscis.gov/sites/default/files/USCIS/Office%20of%20Citizenship/Citizenship%20Resource%20Center%20Site/Publications/100q.pdf, but remember the answers to certain questions about elected officials may change with elections, so make sure you have the most up-to-date information. You can access information on the test, study materials, and practice tests at www.uscis.gov/citizenship/learners/study-test/study-materials-civics-test.

Exceptions to the Test Requirements:

You may not have to take the English test if you are over 50 years old and have lived in the U.S. as an LPR for over 20 years, or if you are over 55 years old and have lived in the U.S. for over 15 years. You may not have to take the civics test if you have certain physical or mental disabilities. For more details, see www.uscis.gov/us-citizenship/citizenship-through-naturalization/exceptions-accommodations. If you are seeking such an exception, you must submit a Form N-648, Medical Certification for Disability Exceptions, along with your N-400, Application for

Naturalization. You may find it at www.uscis.gov/n-648.

USCIS will usually provide you with a notice of your results the same day. However, sometimes USCIS will not be able to make a decision, and may need to continue your case. The officer may then require a second interview, or ask for additional evidence. If USCIS does not need further information, they will either approve your application if you provide evidence that establishes your eligibility, or deny it if your interview, test results, and evidence do not show you are eligible to naturalize.

What Can I Do If USCIS Denies My Application?

If your application was denied, USCIS will provide a written explanation with the reasons for denial. If you think USCIS incorrectly denied your application, you may request a hearing to appeal. You must file a Form N-336, Request for a Hearing on a Decision in Naturalization Proceedings, available at www.uscis.gov/n-336. **You must file this appeal, along with the filing fee, within 30 days of your denial, or the decision will be final.**

What Happens After USCIS Approves My Application?

USCIS will mail you a notice to take the Oath of Allegiance, with the date, time, and location of your oath ceremony. Occasionally, you may be able to take the Oath of Allegiance the same day your application is approved after your interview. If you cannot attend your ceremony, return the notice and explain why you cannot attend, and request a rescheduled ceremony.

During your ceremony, you will take an Oath of Allegiance to the U.S. Remember to bring your green card, because you will turn it in after the ceremony and receive a Certificate of Naturalization, which certifies that you are a naturalized American citizen. Congratulations!

Important! You must still notify USCIS if you change your address after you submit your N-400 application and while you are waiting to complete the process and become a citizen. You must call Customer Service at 1-800-375-5283 (TTY: 1-800-767-1833), and fill out an AR-11, Alien's Change of Address Card, and submit it to USCIS within 10 days of your move. See Chapter 8, "What You Must Do When You Change Your Address," for more details.

How Do I Prove My Status When I Get Citizenship?

You will receive a Form N-550, Certificate of Naturalization, after you take your Oath of Allegiance to the U.S. This proves your status as an American citizen. If you lose this certificate, you must submit Form N-565, Application for Replacement Naturalization/Citizenship Document, available at www.uscis.gov/n-565.

What Should I Do When I Naturalize?

Update Your Social Security Record

After you naturalize, you must update your Social Security record. It is important for Social Security to have updated records on your citizenship. This will make it easier for you to access the benefits and rights to which you are entitled as a U.S. citizen, including Social Security and other government benefits. Wait at least 10 days after your naturalization ceremony, then call Social Security at 1-800-772-1213 or visit www.socialsecurity.gov to make an appointment. Remember to bring your Certificate of Naturalization or U.S. Passport.

Register to Vote

You may now register to vote if you wish to vote in elections. You may do this in person, by mail, at public assistance offices, or when you apply to renew your driver's license. Visit the U.S. Election Assistance Commission online at www.eac.gov.

Apply for a U.S. Passport If You Wish to Travel Abroad

After you naturalize, you are also eligible to apply for a U.S. passport, which will allow you to travel abroad as a U.S. citizen and receive help from U.S. embassies or consulates abroad if you need it. Visit www.travel.state.gov to download the application forms and find the passport acceptance facility near you.

Apply for Your LPR Children Under 18

If you have any children who were born abroad, are lawful permanent residents, and are under 18 on the day you naturalized, they may have automatically become U.S. citizens as well, and you may want to apply for proof of their status. You may apply for a U.S. passport for your child, or apply for a Certificate of Citizenship using Form N-600, Application for Certificate of Citizenship, available at www.uscis.gov/n-600k.

Apply to Sponsor Relatives Abroad to Come to the U.S.

You may now also apply to sponsor additional relatives to come to the U.S. You will be applying for these family members to get green cards. As a U.S. citizen, you may apply to bring your immediate relatives. The "immediate relative" category includes your husband or wife, unmarried children under the age of 21, and parents (as long as you are over 21). These applications are processed immediately and there is no waitlist.

You may also apply to bring other family members who fit into a "family preference category." This category includes your unmarried sons or daughters over the age of 21, married children of any age, and your brothers and sisters (as long as you are over 21). The government has a limited amount of visas available for these family members each year, and they go on a waitlist for family members in each category. The waitlist can be quite long and it can take years. For more information on how to bring your family members who are still abroad to the U.S., please see USCIS's website on sponsoring family members, at www.uscis.gov/green-card/green-card-through-family, and see an immigration lawyer for help.

CHAPTER 12

Traveling Outside of the United States

It is important that you know the risks of traveling outside of the U.S. if you are not a U.S. citizen. Most people reading this guide should not travel outside the U.S. without talking to your lawyer first, because you will risk losing your status. Even lawful permanent residents have restrictions on their travel, which are covered under the LPR supplement.

Important! For anyone planning to "naturalize," or become a U.S. citizen, you should not travel outside the U.S. for more than six months at a time.

Important! If you have committed a crime, you will likely not be able to re-enter the U.S. if you leave. Even if your crime did not make you "deportable," it could make you "inadmissible," which means Immigration will not let you enter the U.S.

Refugees and Asylees

Refugees and asylees must use a refugee travel document, which is a special document that allows refugees and asylees to travel in and out of the U.S. It is also referred to as Advanced Parole for other statuses not covered in this guide.

Important! If you go back to the country you fled, you may lose your legal protective status. It may be impossible for you to ask for legal protective status again.

If you are going to travel outside the U.S., talk to a BIA accredited representative or an immigration lawyer before leaving to make sure that you will not have any problem returning. Also call the embassy or consulate in the countries to which you are traveling to make sure they accept the refugee travel document.

How to Apply for a Refugee Travel Document

You must fill out Form I-131, Application for Travel Document. You can request the most recent version of form I-131 by calling USCIS at 1-800-870-3676 or you can get the form online at www.uscis.gov/i-131. If you can, get help from a BIA accredited organization or an immigration lawyer when you apply for a refugee travel document.

Be sure to carefully read all the instructions on the form. Here are a few things to keep in mind:

- Make sure you include copies of all necessary supporting documents mentioned in the form's instructions.
- The USCIS application has a processing fee. You can get a money order to pay the fee from the post office.
- Keep a photocopy of the completed form for your records. Send the form via certified mail with a return receipt, available at the post office.

- After filing your I-131, USCIS will write you a letter telling you to go to your local Application Support Center for a biometrics appointment. This means they will take your fingerprints. You will need to take two passport-style pictures. You will have to pay a fee.
- There is no way to tell how long it will take to get a refugee travel document. Do not buy airplane tickets until you get your refugee travel document.

Call the USCIS National Customer Service Center at 1-800-375-5283 or look online at www.uscis.gov/i-131 to find out where the form, supporting documents, and processing fee should be sent. You may be able to submit the application online. Go to www.uscis.gov/e-filing to find out if you can file your application online (e-Filing).

Asylum Seekers

Generally, asylum seekers should not travel, especially to countries where you fear persecution, because USCIS will likely assume you have abandoned your asylum application, even if you tell them you have not.

If you need to travel for urgent reasons, you must obtain permission beforehand. This is called Advance Parole. You must fill out Form I-131, Application for Travel Document, and check the box indicating you are applying for an Advance Parole Document that will allow you to return to the U.S. after brief travel abroad. You should consult an attorney before doing this, and should really only do so in urgent situations.

CHAPTER 12

Withholding of Removal and CAT

If you have WOR or protection under the CAT and travel outside of the U.S., **you will not be allowed to come back.**

Traveling in the United States

You do not need a refugee travel document to travel in the U.S., but to travel by plane, train, or bus, you will need a government-issued picture ID. Be sure to carry a copy of your immigration documents with you.

CHAPTER 13

Voting, the Selective Service Requirement, and Joining the Military

Voting

You may want to take part in civic and political activities in the U.S., and may wish to vote. It is very important to understand that **only U.S. citizens can vote in federal elections.** Some state and local governments may allow noncitizens to vote; however this is rare and you should check first with your local government. **If you vote in a federal election before you have U.S. citizenship, you could lose your status, and will never be able to become a citizen.**

Selective Service

All men living in the U.S. between the ages of 18 and 25 are required by law to register with the Military Selective Service System, regardless of immigration status. Men are required to register within 30 days of turning 18. It is important to register. If you do not register, you may be denied benefits, loans, or jobs in the future. It could also make it difficult for you to become a U.S. citizen.

CHAPTER 13

There is not a draft (requirement to fight in war). There has not been a draft in the U.S. since the 1970s; military service has been voluntary (your choice) since then, and is likely to stay that way. The Selective Service is just a backup. Your record will be kept but you will not have to fight in war. If the President and the Congress decide to start a military draft, they will choose who has to fight through a lottery based on birth dates. However, this is highly unlikely.

If a draft is declared and you are called to serve, you can make a claim to be classified as a conscientious objector (CO). This means you do not believe in fighting war for moral or religious reasons. If you were called to serve, you would have to go before your local Selective Service board and explain why you do not believe in fighting.

How to Register

If you have a Social Security number, you can go online to register for Selective Service at https://www.sss.gov/RegVer/wfRegistration.aspx. Or, you can go to any post office and fill out the Selective Service form. Bring your Social Security card. If you do not have a Social Security number, you will have to send a copy of your Social Security card when you get one. When you send it, also put your complete name, date of birth, Selective Service registration number, and current mailing address. You can send it to

Selective Service System
P.O. Box 94636
Palatine, IL 60094-4636

For more information about the Selective Service System go online to www.sss.gov or call 1-888-655-1825.

VOTING, THE SELECTIVE SERVICE REQUIREMENT, AND JOINING THE MILITARY

Joining the Military

Only U.S. citizens and certain lawful permanent residents (LPRs/ green card holders) can join the military. For more information, see www.military.com/join-armed-forces.

CHAPTER 14

The Right to Work

Do You Have the Right to Work?

Rules concerning employment for immigrants in the U.S. are complicated. There are four categories you may fall under: 1) immigrants who are authorized to work as soon as they get their status, without restriction, and do not have to apply for work authorization; 2) immigrants who are authorized to work with their status without restriction, but must apply for a work permit; 3) immigrants who must apply to USCIS for permission to work, and may or may not be granted permission; and 4) those who are unauthorized to work. This section will list all the statuses that fall under each category, but will only discuss the statuses covered in this guide below. Details and instructions for others statuses will be discussed in supplements. Any status not mentioned below is ineligible to work.

Immigrants holding the following statuses or visas are authorized to work as soon as they get their status, without restriction, and do not have to apply with USCIS for a work permit:

- Lawful permanent residents (LPRs)
- Refugees
- Asylees
- Victims of trafficking (T-visa, or certified as a victim of trafficking)
- U-visa (Immigrant victims of crime visa)
- Special Immigrant Visa (SIV)—Iraqi or Afghan translators or employees of the U.S. military government or U.S. government contractor in Iraq or Afghanistan

Immigrants with the following statuses or visas are authorized to work without restriction, but must apply for a work permit before they begin work:

- Parolees (paroled in as refugees) who received work authorization when paroled
- Withholding of removal/deportation
- Deferred enforced departure
- Temporary Protected Status
- Voluntary departure
- Family Unity beneficiaries under LIFE Act
- U-visa including derivatives (family members); U-2, U-3, U-4, and U-5

Immigrants in the following statuses or visas must apply to USCIS for permission to work, and may or may not be granted permission:

- Asylum seekers with pending cases
- Asylum seekers whose cases have been recommended for approval but have not yet received a decision
- Applicants for adjustment of status
- Applicants for suspension of deportation (pre-April 1997)

or cancellation of removal

- Humanitarian or public interest parole
- Deferred action
- Final order of removal but who cannot be removed (including Deferral under CAT)
- Applicant for Temporary Protected Status
- Immediate family members of T-visa recipients holding derivative status (T-2, T-3, T-4, and T-5 holders)

How Do You Show Employers That You Are Eligible to Work?

You must show your employer two documents to work—a photo document that proves your identity and a document that proves you have the legal right to work. If you have an EAD (work permit), you only have to show your EAD. Information on how to apply for an EAD, by status, is provided in the next chapter. The USCIS Form I-9, available at: www.uscis.gov/i-9, has a list of what documents you can show your employer.

If you can, it is best to show your employer that you meet the I-9 requirements without using an immigration document. For example, use your Social Security card and driver's license. Otherwise, they may think your work authorization is limited. If you can satisfy the I-9 requirements with other documents that are on the list of acceptable documents on the I-9 form, the employer is not allowed to require you to show your green card.

Confusion About Employment Authorization

Sometimes employers get confused about your right to work or the documents you need to show. Sometimes they want to see a green card or a work permit, even though you have shown them all the documents they need to see. Some employers use a system on the Internet called E-Verify to check your right to work in the

U.S. They can find E-Verify at www.dhs.gov/e-verify. You can enter your information on E-Verify at www.uscis.gov/everifyselfcheck to know what an employer will see if they check online. You can also go online to www.nilc.org to find a "Know Your Rights About E-Verify" document, available in English and Spanish.

If you or your potential employer have any questions about what documents are needed, you can call the Office of Special Counsel for Immigration-Related Unfair Employment Practices in the Department of Justice. You or your potential employer can call the appropriate toll-free number listed below and talk to a government official who can explain your rights when getting a job.

How to Contact the Office of Special Counsel for Immigration-Related Unfair Employment Practices:

- You should call the Worker Information Hotline: 1-800-255-7688
- The employer should call the Employer Information Hotline: 1-800-255-8155
- E-mail address: osccrt@usdoj.gov
- Website: www.usdoj.gov/crt/osc

Employment Assistance

Refugees, asylees, Cuban-Haitian entrants, victims of trafficking, and SIV holders are eligible to receive Matching Grant and state refugee social services employment assistance. Both are usually administered by refugee resettlement agencies. For information on Matching Grant services, see Chapter 18, "How to Get Public Benefits and Financial Support."

For information on how to apply for your work permit, see the next chapter.

SECTION 3

Basic Services and Needs

This next portion of this guide talks about the basic services you may wish to access to have a better life in the U.S. This section covers topics such as eligibility for and how to get a work permit, Social Security number, state identification (ID) card, health care, financial help, housing, and education. Your status will determine your access to many of these services and programs, and the rules are very complex.

As always, we recommend you use this as a general guide, and consult with a lawyer or expert in the field of the service you seek. It is important to remember that additional services may be available in certain states and the requirements for some of these programs change from state-to-state.

CHAPTER 15

How to Get a Work Permit

What is an "EAD"?
An Employment Authorization Document (EAD) is your work permit. It is not always required to get a job, but it can help prove you have permission to work. It is also useful because it has your photo on it, and you can use it as a photo ID. For information on who has the right to work, and therefore who has the right to apply for an EAD, please see Chapter 14, "Right to Work."

How Do I Apply for an EAD?

All applicants who are eligible for employment authorization must fill out Form I-765, Application for Employment Authorization. See the USCIS website's page on work permits to download the application, view instructions on filling out the form, and find out where to send it: www.uscis.gov/i-765. There is a filing fee, but you do not have to pay for your first EAD (you must pay for replacements) if you are in one of the following categories: refugee, asylee, asylum seeker, granted withholding of removal, parolee, VAWA self-petitioner, U-visa holder, or trafficking victim.

Additionally, you must submit the following:

- Copy of your I-94 Arrival Departure Record
- Copy of a government-issued ID, such as a passport or state ID card
- Two identical 2x2 color photographs of yourself, taken within 30 days of the application, with your name and A-number written on the back.

Following are special instructions based on your immigration status.

Refugees

As a refugee, your I-94 (the Arrival and Departure Card that you received when you arrived at the U.S. airport) gives you the right to work. You do not need to apply for an EAD. USCIS will issue you an EAD soon after your arrival, and your Resettlement Agency will deliver it to you. However, you do not need this to apply for or accept a job. If you do not receive your EAD, ask your Resettlement Agency for help. If you do not have your EAD yet, and your employer does not understand that your I-94 gives you permission to work, or if you otherwise have trouble with your employer understanding you are authorized to work, see Chapter 14, "Right to Work."

Once you get your EAD, it may have an expiration date on it. This means only that the document must be renewed, not that the authorization to work has expired. Your first EAD is free, but you must pay for the replacements.

You should also apply for a Social Security number and card, which you must have if you accept employment. See Chapter 16, "How to Get a Social Security Number."

Asylees

If you are granted asylum you may work right away, and you do not need to apply for an EAD. However, you may choose to get an EAD for convenience or identification purposes. If a potential employer questions your ability to work, you can print a document from the USCIS website (www.uscis.gov/sites/default/files/USCIS/Resources/D2en.pdf) that explains that asylees are automatically authorized to work and do not need an EAD, and show it to your employer. Or, you may want to fill out the EAD application just to make things easier. If so, fill out Form I-765, Application for Employment Authorization, as described above.

Once you get your EAD, it may have an expiration date on it. This means only that the document must be renewed, not that the authorization to work has expired. Your first EAD is free, but you must pay for the replacements.

You should also apply for a Social Security number and card, which you must have if you accept employment. See Chapter 16, "How to Get a Social Security Number."

Asylum Seekers

The rules about when an asylum seeker becomes eligible for employment are complicated. As an asylum seeker, you cannot apply for employment authorization at the same time you apply for asylum. If no decision has been made about your asylum application after 150 days, you can apply for work authorization. USCIS has 30 days to approve or deny the application, so you could be eligible to receive your work permit 180 days after you applied for asylum. If you apply before 150 days, your application will be denied. If you are given a "recommended approval for a grant of asylum" before the 150 days, you can apply for an EAD immediately. To apply for a work permit, fill out Form I-765, Application for Employment Authorization, using the instructions above. Additionally, you should submit the following documents. If you need help figuring out which of these documents you have or are able to submit, seek help from a BIA accredited representative or lawyer.

- A copy of the USCIS acknowledgement mailer you received in the mail, or any other evidence your Form I-589 (asylum application) was filed with USCIS, or
- Evidence you filed a Form I-589 with an Immigration Judge, or
- Evidence your asylum application remains under administrative or judicial review, or
- Evidence you have "lodged" your asylum claim for EAD purposes (more below).

The Asylum EAD Clock

USCIS and EOIR use something referred to as the "asylum EAD clock" to determine when the 180-day period is up and the applicant is eligible. It starts when the applicant files or lodges a complete asylum application. It stops running (so days stop being counted for credit towards eligibility) when an applicant or the applicant's lawyer causes any delay. Once the delay has been resolved, the clock should restart.

Asylum seekers often end up waiting years for a work permit, because many unexpected and common actions count as "applicant-caused" delay, some of which are necessary to build a case, such as requests for continuance (asking for more time) to find a lawyer, acquire evidence, work on a case; or rejecting an initial hearing date that the applicant cannot attend. Unfortunately, EOIR does not consider these delays to be "resolved" (allowing the clock to restart) until the next hearing date. So if an asylum seeker is given a hearing in 14 days and asks for additional time to find a lawyer, or the lawyer asks for reasonable time to work on the case, the court may not schedule the next hearing for months or years. The EAD clock does not run this entire time, so applicants remain ineligible for work permits.

Additionally, increasing backlogs in immigration court have led to asylum seekers being scheduled for initial hearings months and sometimes years down the line, which means they have not had the opportunity to file an asylum application to start the EAD clock.

Because of all the problems the asylum clock caused, a recent settlement in a class action court case determined that USCIS and EOIR must change some of their rules and practices, to make it easier for asylum seekers to get work permits. Before the lawsuit, the clock only started running once an applicant filed a complete asylum application with an Immigration Judge in a hearing, which often took months or years due to massive backlogs in immigration court. The lawsuit created a process called "lodging" that allows an asylum seeker to submit an asylum application to the immigration court clerk before their hearing, for purposes of starting the EAD clock only, so the applicant does not have to wait for a hearing to start accumulating time on the clock.

How to "Lodge" an Asylum Application

Not everyone may lodge an application. Only asylum seekers who plan to file an asylum application defensively (who are in removal proceedings in Immigration Court), but have not yet done so, may lodge. You may not lodge if you are applying affirmatively through

USCIS (so those who are not in removal proceedings), or if USCIS referred your case to an Immigration Judge (because you already have an application on file, so your clock started). Those who are eligible to lodge may only do so once, and must do so before filing in Immigration Court. Be sure to lodge your application at the correct Immigration Court, where your case is pending.

There are two ways to lodge an asylum application.

- Applicants can take the complete asylum application to their Immigration Court's public window and lodge in person with the clerk.
- Alternatively, applicants can lodge a complete asylum application by mail or courier. If submitting by mail or courier, you **must** include the following:
    - o A self-addressed, stamped envelope (or comparable return delivery packaging), AND
    - o A cover page, or a prominent note at the top of the first page of the asylum application, stating it is being submitted for the purpose of lodging.

The court clerk will stamp the application "lodged not filed," return the application to the asylum seeker, and will give the asylum seeker a 180-day Asylum EAD Clock Notice. The clerk sends notification to DHS that an application was lodged, and the EAD clock starts.

Important! A lodged application is not considered filed! The Immigration Court does not keep a copy of the application. **You must still file a complete asylum application in Immigration Court during your hearing.** Lodging is only for the purposes of notifying DHS that an applicant will be filing an application in the future, so the applicant can start accumulating the 180 days required to be eligible for a work permit.

HOW TO GET A WORK PERMIT

Note: Make sure your application is complete. This means all questions on the I-589 must be answered, it must be signed, and must include any supporting evidence as required on the application. However, you can still submit additional evidence later at your asylum interview or court hearing if you do not have everything when you wish to lodge the application.

<u>Other Important Changes to EAD Eligibility and Remedies from the Settlement</u>

Some asylum seekers are in "expedited," or fast, proceedings, in which judges must complete the case within 180 days. (You might be in expedited proceedings if you originally applied affirmatively with USCIS and they referred your case to Immigration Court, or if you are in removal proceedings and have not requested a continuance.) In expedited cases, judges previously often gave individual (merits) hearing dates within 14 days of the initial master calendar hearing, which was not enough time for asylum seekers to find a lawyer or prepare a case. Requests for more time to find a lawyer or prepare caused the clock to stop. Recognizing that 14 days is not enough time to find a lawyer or prepare a case, the settlement mandated that judges must give non-detained clients in expedited proceedings hearings that are at least 45 days after their master calendar, to give more time to prepare the case, so applicants do not have to ask for a later date and further delay EAD eligibility. However, applicants in expedited proceedings must accept this date, or the clock will stop due to applicant-caused delay.

Another change is that if you lost your case before a judge and appealed to the BIA, now your "asylum clock" will start up again if the BIA sends your case back to the judge to make a new decision. Unfortunately, it still stops when you lose your case, and does not start again until the appeal is complete at the BIA, and only if the BIA sends it back to Immigration Court. If this happens, however, you will be credited for all the days you lost while your appeal was pending.

Additionally, if you miss a hearing (which you should not do unless you have an emergency!) USCIS will mail you a letter giving you 45 days to give a good reason. (You still must have a good reason, like an emergency out of your control.)

Finally, judges are now required to let asylum seekers and their lawyers know the consequences of asking for case delays for various reasons, and whether it will stop the "asylum clock" and delay the work permit process.

How to Address These EAD Clock Problems

Most of the settlement only applies to problems experienced after the date of the settlement, December 3, 2013. If you experienced delay in your work authorization due to any of the following problems after that date, you should ask a lawyer if you are eligible to file a claim under the settlement, which could correct any mistakes and make you eligible for an EAD if you were incorrectly denied:

- If the Immigration Court did not give you a 180-day Asylum EAD Clock Notice when you filed or lodged your claim, or if USCIS referred your claim to Immigration Court and did not give you the Notice;
- If the Immigration Court clerk did not stamp your lodged application "lodged not filed" and return the application to you, or otherwise prevented you from lodging, or if USCIS did not use the lodging date to start the clock;
- If your EAD clock stopped because you did not accept an expedited hearing date;
- If an applicant in affirmative proceedings missed a USCIS

appointment, and USCIS did not mail a Failure to Appear warning letter and give the applicant 45 days to show good cause;
- If the BIA remanded (sent the case back to an Immigration Judge) a case on appeal, but the EAD application was denied because DHS did not credit the time missed.

Other Common Types of Delays

Courts consider many other common issues to be applicant-caused, which therefore stop the EAD clock. Delays without good cause in getting fingerprinting, and delays caused if an applicant in affirmative proceedings cannot find an interpreter to bring to their USCIS interview (Immigration Court provides interpreters to defensive applicants) will stop the clock. If USCIS or the court requests more evidence, the clock will stop from the time of the request to the next hearing, which could be very far in the future. It will also stop if the applicant delays proceedings by requesting time to gather additional evidence. Requests to transfer USCIS interviews to a different office, even if the applicant moves, will cause delay. Likewise, requests to transfer a case to a different Immigration Court can cause delay; however, the clock will not stop if the two hearing locations share administrative control of the case. The clock sometimes stops if a defensive asylum seeker "contests the charges of removability" (argues he does not agree that he is removable), or applies for another form of relief, such as a T- or U-visa.

How to Address These EAD Clock Problems

Although you should try to avoid unnecessary delays, sometimes delays are necessary and offer the best chance for success, such as applying for another form of relief. You cannot address these other common types of delays through the settlement; however, your lawyer may be able to argue that the clock should not stop for certain types of delays.

CHAPTER 15

You and your lawyer may take the following steps if you have problems or questions about the clock:

If you are in affirmative proceedings (your case is before USCIS)

- All questions on the EAD clock should be directed to the points of contact (POCs) at the Asylum Office with jurisdiction over the case. They can be found on the USCIS Asylum Division's page on Asylum Employment Authorization and Clock Contacts, at www.uscis.gov/sites/default/files/files/nativedocuments/EAD_and_KLOK_POCs_4_30_14.pdf.

If you are in removal proceedings and are applying defensively (your case is in Immigration Court)

- Address the issue to the judge in your hearing.
- If the judge did not adequately address the issue, raise it with the court administrator in writing.
- If the court administrator did not adequately address the issue, contact the Assistant Chief Immigration Judge in writing.
- If your case is on appeal (during which time the clock will not run) and you believe more time should have accumulated before the clock stopped when Immigration Court rejected your case, contact the EIOR Office of General Counsel in writing.

You may find the contact information for the above offices on EOIR's Immigration Court Listing page, at www.justice.gov/eoir/sibpages/ICadr.htm.

If you think you were unable to get your work permit in the past because of any of the problems described above, ask a BIA accredited representative or lawyer for help. You can find an immigration legal services provider near you by consulting the directory in Chapter 27. You may also contact the Legal Action Center at asylumclock@immcouncil.org, or the Northwest Immigrant Rights Project at asylumclock@nwirp.org.

Withholding of Removal (INA and CAT)

If you are granted withholding of removal, you are eligible to work, but must apply to USCIS for documentation first. File Form I-765, according to the instructions above. You must also file your judge's order. You should apply for a new EAD 90 days before your current one expires.

Deferral Under CAT

If you were granted deferral of removal under the Convention Against Torture, you are not guaranteed employment authorization. You must apply to USCIS, and must have compelling reasons for needing employment, such as the need to support a spouse or children in the U.S.

File Form I-765 according to the above instructions, along with the following information:

- Copy of your order of supervision
- Request for employment authorization that may be based on one of the following:
    - Existence of husband, wife, or children in the U.S. who depend on your for support,
    - Economic necessity, or
    - Estimated time before you can be removed from the U.S.

You must explain the above in detail. It is helpful to provide documents to support your request.

What to Do if You Have Applied for an EAD, But Have Not Heard Anything Yet

If you have been waiting for longer than the expected processing time of 30 days and you have not recently had any type of notice or update from ICE, you can call the USCIS National Customer Service Center at 1-800-375-5283. Have your A-number available. You can also check your case status online. Go to www.uscis.gov and click on "Check Your Case Status."

Income Tax

If you are working, you will need to file an income tax form. Your employers will send you a form called a W-2 or 1099. This form shows how much money you have made during the year. Be sure to update past employers for whom you worked during that year with your current address so they can send your W-2 or 1099. If you have questions about filing your income tax forms, ask friends or family for local organizations that can help you with your taxes. There are private organizations that help to fill out these forms, but they charge a large fee. You may be able to find a free tax preparer by calling the Volunteer Income Tax Assistance Program at 1-800-906-9886 or going online to www.irs.gov/Individuals/Free-Tax-Return-Preparation-for-You-by-Volunteers.

It is very important to pay your taxes. If you do not pay the taxes you owe, it will cause you problems later when you apply for your green card or U.S. citizenship, or try to sponsor a family member. You can be sent to jail, have your paycheck taken away or have property like a car taken from you for not paying.

HOW TO GET A WORK PERMIT

For more information on income taxes go online to www.irs.gov or call 1-800-829-1040.

CHAPTER 16

How to Get a Social Security Number

What Is a Social Security Number (SSN), and Why Do I Need One?

A Social Security number (SSN) is a 9-digit number the U.S. government assigns to U.S. citizens, lawful permanent residents, and other lawfully present individuals. It is important because you need it to access certain benefits and rights you may be entitled to. For example, if you are authorized to work, you will need to get a SSN before you can get a job, and you may need it to access certain government services and benefits. The government uses it to track your income from working to determine how much tax you owe, as you must pay tax if you work. Your SSN is unique to you, and you should be very careful to keep your Social Security card safe and to not let other people know your SSN, because it could put you at risk for identity theft. Identity theft occurs when someone steals your personal information and uses it without your permission. See Chapter 22, "How to Keep Your Money Safe and Make It Grow," for more information and tips to avoid identity theft.

If you are eligible to work in the U.S., you are eligible to get a SSN.

CHAPTER 16

If you are eligible for a SSN, you should apply for and receive a Social Security card, which contains your SSN. Instructions for applying are below. You may be eligible for a SSN under other limited circumstances described below. To read more about SSNs for non-U.S. citizens, see www.ssa.gov/pubs/EN-05-10096.pdf.

There are three kinds of Social Security cards, and your immigration status and employment eligibility determine the type of card you receive.

- The most common kind shows your name and SSN, allows you to work without restriction, and is what most U.S. citizens and those admitted on a permanent basis receive.
- The second type, a restricted card, shows your name and SSN, and says, "VALID FOR WORK ONLY WITH DHS AUTHORIZATION." This type is issued to people who are lawfully admitted on a temporary basis (including those with the possibility of later adjusting status to LPR).
- The third type, which is also restricted and very rare, shows your name and SSN, and says, "NOT VALID FOR EMPLOYMENT." This type of card is issued to noncitizens who are lawfully admitted to the U.S. and do not have work authorization, but either have a valid non-work reason for needing a number, or need a number because of a federal law requiring a SSN to receive a benefit or service, such as TANF, Medicaid, or food stamps. (These benefits are covered more thoroughly in Chapters 18 and 19.)

You can still receive many services without a SSN. You do not need a SSN to get a driver's license, register for school, get private health insurance, or apply for school lunch programs or subsidized housing. However, employers, banks, and departments of motor vehicles may ask for your SSN. Local branches of social services offices will use your SSN to see what benefits you qualify for. When you apply for federal financial aid to study for college, schools will ask for your SSN. The federal government will also use your SSN to determine how much to give you in Social Security benefits when you reach full retirement age or become disabled and no longer have income. For these reasons, it is best to get one if you are eligible.

If you are not authorized to work in the U.S. or otherwise do not qualify for a SSN, but you need a number for tax reporting or filing purposes, you can apply for an Individual Taxpayer Identification Number (ITIN) from the Internal Revenue Service (IRS).

Important! An ITIN does not make you eligible to work or receive Social Security benefits; it is only used for federal tax reporting purposes. If you are confused as to whether you might need an ITIN, see a BIA accredited representative or a lawyer who offers free or low-cost services.

How Do I Get a SSN?

To obtain a Social Security number, you must visit a Social Security office in person to complete and sign an application for a Social Security number. Find your local office at www.socialsecurity.gov/locator. For more information, you may call 1-800-772-1213. For the deaf or hearing-impaired, call the TTY number, 1-800-325-0778.

You will have to complete Form SS-5, Application for a Social Security Card. You may find this form at www.ssa.gov/online/ss-5.pdf. You must then take the form to an office to submit it. You must also show original documents or copies certified by the issuing agency showing 1) U.S. citizenship or immigration status (including DHS permission to work), 2) age, and 3) identity.

1. You can show several types of documents to prove your immigration status, like your I-94, your work permit, or your judge's decision or court order. For a list of documents you can use to prove your status, view the Social Security Administration's list at www.ssa.gov/pubs/EN-05-10096.pdf, and see Chapter 7, "Case Status and Proof of Status."
2. To show your age, you may submit your birth certificate, U.S. hospital record of your birth, passport, or U.S. Immigration document.
3. To prove your identity, you must submit a document that is current, shows your name, identifying information, and preferably a photograph. If you don't have the documents the Social Security Administration (SSA) requests, they may ask to see one of the following: employee ID card, school ID card, health insurance card (not including Medicare), U.S. military ID card, adoption decree, life insurance policy, or marriage document in the event of a name change.

After you have submitted your form, ask for a receipt, which is the proof that you applied.

How Much Does It Cost?

There is no charge for a SSN or card. If anyone tries to charge you, you can report them by calling 1-800-269-0271.

What If I Do Not Receive My Social Security Card?

You should receive your Social Security card in the mail within 10 days. If you do not, you can either return to your local office to ask, or call 1-800-772-1213. When you go, take the documents you originally presented as evidence, or have them available if you call.

If you have already applied for a SSN but your employer needs to verify your name and SSN immediately, they can use the online SSN Verification Service at www.ssa.gov/employer/ssnv.htm or call the Telephone Number Employer Verification service, which is explained at www.ssa.gov/employer/documents/TNEV.pdf.

How Do I Get an ITIN?

Remember, you only can apply for an ITIN if you are not eligible for a SSN. To obtain an Individual Taxpayer Identification Number, visit the IRS in person or call 1-800-TAXFORM (1-800-829-3676) to complete your application form.

You will fill out a Form W-7, Application for IRS Individual Taxpayer Identification Number, which you can find at www.irs.gov/pub/irs-pdf/fw7.pdf. Mail your completed application to:

Internal Revenue Service
Austin Service Center
ITIN Operation
P.O. Box 149342
Austin, TX 78714-9342

You may also apply using the services of an IRS-authorized Acceptance Agent (listed at www.irs.gov/Individuals/Acceptance-Agent-Program) or visit an IRS Taxpayer Assistance Center (TAC) instead of mailing your information to the IRS in Austin. TACs provide in-person help with ITIN applications on a walk-in or appointment basis, and you can find the list of centers at www.irs.gov/uac/TAC-Locations-Where-In-Person-Document-Verification-is-Provided. If you need help, you can call the IRS at 1-800-829-1040.

When you submit the W-7, attach a valid federal income tax return if you have one, unless you qualify for an exception, and include your original proof of identity or copies certified by issuing agency and foreign status documents. A full list of acceptable documents is available at http://www.irs.gov/Individuals/Revised-Application-Standards-for-ITINs.

You should receive a letter from the IRS assigning your ITIN within six weeks after you applied. If you have not heard from the IRS six weeks after applying, call the IRS at 1-800-829-1040.

Note that as of January 2013, ITINs expire every five years. If you require an ITIN and remain ineligible for a SSN, you must reapply for an ITIN every five years.

Important! The Social Security office will check your immigration status. If you are not authorized to work and receive a SSN or ITIN for non-work purposes, but then use it to work, the SSA will report you to DHS, and you could be arrested, and could possibly be deported.

Am I Eligible for a SSN?
Below you will find details on your eligibility for a SSN according to your status.

Refugees & Asylees

As a refugee or an asylee, you are eligible immediately to apply for a SSN. See Chapter 7, "Case Status and Proof of Status," for a list of documents you can use to prove your status. Remember that some I-94s say "employment authorized" and some do not. This does not mean anything, as all refugees and asylees are immediately authorized to work, and your I-94 does not need to say that you are authorized to work.

HOW TO GET A SOCIAL SECURITY NUMBER

Asylum Seekers

You can apply for a SSN, but will receive a restricted Social Security card, which will state either "VALID FOR WORK ONLY WITH DHS AUTHORIZATION," or "NOT VALID FOR WORK," depending on whether you are eligible to work. See Chapter 7 for a list of documents you can use to prove your status.

It can be difficult for asylum seekers to get a SSN, because the Social Security Administration (SSA) requires two forms of ID, and often ICE (Immigrations and Customs Enforcement) holds asylum seekers' passports while they are in immigration proceedings. Usually, ICE will not give your passport back until the case is finished. If ICE has your passport or other ID, sometimes your lawyer can get ICE to agree to make a photocopy for its records and return the original to you to take to SSA.

Withholding of Removal (INA and CAT)

Because your status is not considered permanent, you are ineligible for the most common type of Social Security card. However, if you are authorized for employment, you will be eligible for the second type of card, which reads, "VALID FOR WORK ONLY WITH DHS AUTHORIZATION."

If for some reason you are not authorized for employment (see Chapter 14, "Right to Work"), you will only be eligible for the third kind of Social Security card, which reads, "NOT VALID FOR WORK." if you are granted withholding under the INA. You will not be eligible if you are issued withholding under CAT. This is because those granted withholding under the INA are considered "qualified immigrants" for purposes of benefits eligibility (see Chapters 18 and 19 on benefits), but those granted withholding under CAT are not.

Deferral Under CAT

Because your status is not considered permanent, you are ineligible for the most common type of Social Security card. However, if you are approved for a work permit, you may qualify for a restricted Social Security card, which reads, "VALID FOR WORK ONLY WITH DHS AUTHORIZATION." It is unlikely that you will be eligible for many benefits, but in the event that you are, you may be eligible for the third kind of Social Security card, which reads, "NOT VALID FOR WORK."

CHAPTER 17

How to Get a State ID Card

ID is short for identification. A state ID card is a helpful document. You can show it to employers, landlords, banks, and other businesses to prove who you are. The card will show your photograph and signature. It will show information about you, including your address, date of birth, sex, eye color, hair color, height, and weight. Many immigrants find it helpful to get a state ID card, even though it can be difficult, because unlike your I-94 or other forms of ID, your state ID card does not mention your citizenship or how long you have been in the U.S.

How Do I Get An ID?

Not everyone is eligible to get an ID. In most states, you should be eligible if you are a lawful permanent resident, refugee, asylee, parolee, SIJS, Cuban-Haitian entrant, SIV holder, or if you have a T-visa or U-visa. It will cost money to get a state ID. Each state has different rules about getting an ID card.

Call your local Department of Motor Vehicles (DMV) office to know what documents you will need to obtain a state ID card. You can locate the nearest DMV office in the phone book or on the Internet. The DMV may have a different name in your state. It may be called the "Motor Vehicle Administration" or the "Division of Motor Vehicles" or something else. Ask someone to help you find the right office.

Depending on your state, you may also be allowed to get a driver's license. This will be expensive and will involve taking driving classes and passing a driving test. **You cannot drive in the U.S. unless you have a driver's license. If you do drive without a license, you could be arrested. You also cannot drink alcohol and drive while you are still under the influence of alcohol, because it is dangerous. Driving without a license and driving while under the influence of alcohol can both lead to your deportation.** Because it takes a long time to learn to drive and obtain your license, you may want to get a state ID first, and worry about driving later.

Important! The paperwork to get your driver's license or other state ID card is long and confusing. There are many questions that ask you to "check" (√) or mark boxes that ask confusing questions. One asks if you would like to vote. **Do not check this box.** If you do, you will be registered to vote, which is illegal for noncitizens. If you register to vote before you are a citizen, you may not be allowed to become a citizen! It is best to take someone like your lawyer or a friend who is an American citizen and who is fluent in English to help you.

What If I Have Problems Getting My State ID Card?

People who work at the DMV may not understand your immigration status, or what documents are required for your status. They may tell you that you do not have the right documents. Ask them to write down which documents you need, why your documents do not meet the requirements, and their name and office phone number.

HOW TO GET A STATE ID CARD

People who work at the DMV may not understand that if your status is indefinite, you should be able to get an ID. Getting an ID can be difficult even for U.S. citizens. Try to be patient. If they still do not understand, ask someone at a refugee or immigrant agency to explain it to them. The refugee or immigrant agency can write a letter to the DMV.

Tip: Certain refugee agencies can issue certification documents if you enroll in their program. The certification includes a photo ID along with a letter verifying that this is a federally recognized ID. This is different in each state and with each agency. See Chapter 25, "Directory of Resettlement Agencies (RAs)," for help if you are a refugee or asylee, or Chapter 27, "Directory of Immigration Legal Services Providers," if you are in another status.

CHAPTER 18

How to Get Public Benefits and Financial Support

Introduction

You may need money and help to find a job and a place to live when you first arrive in the U.S. or are released from immigration detention. You may be eligible for some forms of government-funded assistance. The types of assistance you are eligible for depend on your status, as well as other factors, and the rules are very complicated. They also depend on whether the benefits come from the federal government or the state government. This section will explain some of those rules, many of which also apply to medical care, which is covered in the next chapter. Financial and medical assistance are referred to as "benefits," because they will help you with important financial and medical needs, and most benefits do not require you to pay the money back.

CHAPTER 18

Note: The National Immigration Law Center (NILC) has expertise in the area of benefits and healthcare for immigrants, and has published a wealth of detailed information.

Please visit **http://nilc.org** for excellent resources and information on access and eligibility for various types of benefits. Please note that NILC does not provide individual legal representation or advice, but serves as a resource on access to benefits and healthcare issues.

In 1996, Congress passed several laws that made it more difficult for immigrants to get benefits. They created two classes of immigrants: **"qualified" and "not qualified"** for benefits purposes. **Qualified immigrants include the following statuses:**

- LPRs (green card holders)
- Refugees
- Asylees
- Withholding of removal (*only under the INA, not under CAT)
- Conditional entrants (what refugees were called before 1980)
- Persons paroled into the U.S. for at least one year
- Cuban and Haitian entrants
- Certain battered (abused) immigrants and their children and/or parents (VAWA self-petitioners – see VAWA supplement for specifics)
- Certain trafficking victims
- SIV (Special Immigrant Visas for Iraqis and Afghans) recipients (this status was included in later legislation)

All other immigrants are not qualified, and may be ineligible for most benefits except for emergency medical aid, immunizations and care for communicable diseases, and certain short-term, in-kind urgent aid described below under the section on benefits available to all immigrants.

Limited Access to "Federal Means-Tested Benefits"

Even many qualified immigrants may be excluded from a lot of benefits. If you came to the U.S. **after August 22, 1996,** you may subject to a "5-year bar," which prevents you from getting certain federal benefits until you have been in your status for five years. There are five types of benefits, known as "means-tested benefits," that impose a five year or longer waiting period for many "qualified" immigrants:

- **Medicaid** (except for emergency Medicaid, which is always available)
- **CHIP** (Children's Health Insurance Program)
- **TANF** (Temporary Assistance for Needy Families, but your state will probably have a different name for it)
- **SNAP** for adults (Supplemental Nutrition Assistance Program, or food stamps)
- **SSI** (Supplemental Security Income)

However, there are exceptions to that rule. **Several groups can get the above benefits as soon as they arrive (or are granted any of the following statuses):**

- Refugees
- Asylees

- Withholding of removal (only under the INA, not under CAT)
- Trafficking victims
- SIV (Special Immigrant Visas for Iraqis and Afghans)
- Cuban-Haitian entrants
- Certain Amerasian immigrants
- "Qualified" immigrant veterans, active duty military, and their spouses and children

The major groups of immigrants who are "qualified" but are subject to the 5-year bar are LPRs, VAWA recipients (battered or abused immigrant spouses, children, or sometimes parents), and parolees of more than one year (with some exceptions for specific benefits, noted in the sections of this chapter).

Note: SSI and SNAP (food stamps) are called "federally-specified" programs, which means that, even though you must apply through a state social services agency, the federal government runs these programs, and uses the same rules in each state across the country. This means the rules about who is eligible for SSI and SNAP are the same throughout the U.S.

However, other programs known as "federally-designated" programs, which include TANF, Medicaid, CHIP, and some other Title XX Social Services Block Grant services, are administered differently by each state. This means each state makes its own rules (within federal guidelines) about who is eligible for these programs, so the rules may be different in different states. Because of this, some states provide such benefits to "qualified" immigrants without a waiting period, and may also provide benefits to "non-qualified" immigrants as well. **This means even if you are "non-qualified," or you are "qualified" but subject to the 5-year federal bar, you**

might be eligible for some benefits in your state immediately. It also means that for certain programs, even if you are federally eligible, there is a chance your state could deny them (but the state cannot deny benefits to those exempt from the 5-year bar like refugees and asylees.) **So it is important to read about each program, and especially check with your state social services office or local advocates to learn what benefits might be available to immigrants in your state or county.**

Federal Public Benefits Available to All Qualified Immigrants

Some other types of benefits, just known as "federal public benefits," are available to all "qualified immigrants," with no restrictions and no 5-year bar. They count as federal public benefits if they are paid directly to an individual, household, or family.

These benefits include loans, contracts, grants, and licenses provided or funded by a U.S. government agency. They also include other benefits (not listed above in the "federal means-tested" category) such as retirement, unemployment, health, disability, welfare, post-secondary education, assisted housing, public housing, and food assistance provided by a U.S. government agency. Ask your state social services agency for details.

Basic Emergency Benefits Available to All Immigrants, Regardless of Status

Non-qualified immigrants, including undocumented immigrants, may be eligible for the following, regardless of status:

- Emergency Medicaid
- Immunizations/treatment of communicable diseases
- School breakfasts and lunches
- WIC (food assistance program for "Women, Infants, and Children")
- Short-term noncash emergency disaster assistance
- Other in-kind services necessary to protect life/safety (as long as no income qualifications are required for eligibility), including:
    - Child/adult protective services
    - Federal programs that address weather emergencies & homelessness
    - Shelters for domestic violence victims, runaway children, and the homeless
    - Soup kitchens
    - Community food banks
    - Meals-On-Wheels
    - Medical, public health, & mental health services necessary to protect public safety
    - Violence and abuse prevention
    - Disability/substance abuse services necessary to protect life/safety
    - Programs that safeguard children, workers, and community residents.

In some states, prenatal care may be available regardless of status, and a few states or counties offer healthcare to children or to other groups, regardless of their status. Additionally, if federal funds are provided to a state as a block grant to a hospital, shelter, or other services agency, they are not considered federal public benefits, and should be available to everyone, regardless of status.

Important! For some immigrants, accepting cash welfare (like SSI and TANF) can create problems with USCIS that can prevent you from staying in the U.S. permanently, if the government is worried you will become a "public charge," which means someone permanently dependent on the government to survive. This does *not* apply to refugees, asylees, asylum seekers, trafficking victims (T-visa holders or applicants), U-visa holders or applicants, SIV holders, or SIJS. USCIS understands and accepts that certain groups of vulnerable immigrants who are not being sponsored by a relative may sometimes need help to rebuild their lives in a new country, and therefore does not apply the rules on public charges to them. If you are not in one of these excepted groups, check with a lawyer or BIA-recognized organization.

Important! As you can see, it is hard for many immigrants, even those with green cards or other lawful statuses, to get benefits, and much more difficult if you are waiting for approval (like an asylum seeker), or if you have no status at all. Remember that **once you become a U.S. citizen, you become eligible for all of the same benefits as American citizens,** and restrictions or wait times based on immigration status no longer apply. **Therefore, it is very important that you "adjust your status" to gain LPR (green card) status as soon as you are eligible,** because once you are an LPR, you can apply for citizenship in five years. Once you naturalize, you will have the same access to benefits as other American citizens.

Note on Where to Apply and Interpretation

You can apply for most of these benefits at the Department of Social Services (a government agency) in your city or town. All agencies that are part of social services departments are required by law to provide you with an interpreter if you request one.

CHAPTER 18

PUBLIC BENEFITS PROGRAMS: HELP WITH CASH AND FOOD

The Matching Grant Program

Important Deadline: If you wish to participate in the Matching Grant Program, you must do so within 31 days after you become eligible! This opportunity for valuable help will expire after 31 days.

Who is Eligible for the Matching Grant Program?
Refugees, asylees, Cuban-Haitian entrants, trafficking victims, SIV holders, and certain Amerasians who can show proof of status are eligible to receive the Matching Grant if they are able and willing to work and show a financial need.

You are *not* eligible if you already receive public cash assistance such as RCA (Refugee Cash Assistance), SSI (Supplemental Security Income), or TANF (Temporary Assistance for Needy Families). (TANF will likely have a different name in your state.)

However, you *may be* eligible to receive SNAP (Supplemental Nutrition Assistance Program, or food stamps), CHIP (Children's Health Insurance Program), RMA (Refugee Medical Assistance) or other public or health benefits at the same time. Each of these programs has its own criteria, so you must check with your state agency to verify your eligibility.

What is the Matching Grant Program?
The Matching Grant Program helps certain groups become self-sufficient (able to support themselves) within six months of being in the U.S. The program helps you find a job through job placement

services. It also offers case management to help you adjust to life in a new society. Services **may** include case management, English classes, job training and recertification, help finding a job, cash allowance, and other support services that assist in adjusting to living in the U.S.

The Matching Grant Program helps you to pay rent at least for your first four months in the program, or until you get a job—whichever happens first. Once you get your first paycheck, rent, utilities, and cash assistance ends. However, you may be able to receive the other Matching Grant services for up to six months from the time you first become enrolled. The Matching Grant will end if your job makes you self-sufficient before the six-month period is over. If you cooperate with the self-sufficiency plan developed with your case manager, you will get $200 per month for each adult and $40 for each child per month in your family.

How to Apply for the Matching Grant Program

The Matching Grant Program is run by certain refugee resettlement agencies and nongovernmental organizations (NGOs). You can find participating agencies in the Directory of Resettlement Agencies (RAs) in the back of this guide. You must apply through the agency that is in your state.

Important! You must enroll within 31 days after becoming eligible. The date of eligibility for Matching Grant services is counted from the date of arrival into the country for refugees and Amerasians; the date of the grant of asylum for asylees; the date a Cuban-Haitian becomes an entrant; the date of the certification of eligibility letter for victims of severe forms of trafficking; and the date an SIV arrives in the U.S. or the date of adjustment of status if applying for SIV status within the U.S.

Wilson-Fish Program

Wilson-Fish is an alternative to the Matching Grant program that exists in 13 states. You cannot participate in both Matching Grant and Wilson-Fish. The rules are the same. ORR currently funds Wilson-Fish programs that operate throughout twelve states: Alabama, Alaska, Colorado, Idaho, Kentucky, Louisiana, Massachusetts, Nevada, North Dakota, South Dakota, Tennessee, Vermont, plus San Diego County, CA. You must apply within 31 days of arriving in the U.S. or receiving your status.

Refugee Cash Assistance (RCA)

What is Refugee Cash Assistance?

RCA provides short-term financial assistance to childless adults while they look for a job. If you qualify for this program and receive benefits, you will not need to pay this money back. If you are approved for RCA, the process may be different in each state. Some states send a check each month in the mail. Other states send a letter giving you an appointment to go to the social services office. At your appointment, you will get an Electronic Benefits Transfer (EBT) card and learn how to use the card. The EBT card allows you to withdraw money from automatic teller machines (ATMs), and to buy certain food from some supermarkets. Stores that accept the card often have a sign. If you do not see a sign, ask if the store accepts the card.

Who is Eligible?

Except in rare cases, RCA is only for single adults or childless couples who do not have any income or who have very low income. You are eligible if you are a refugee, asylee, trafficking victim, SIV holder, Cuban-Haitian entrant, Amerasian, or conditional entrant. You become eligible for RCA as soon as you arrive as a refugee or parolee or when you receive your status.

How Long Can I Use RCA?

You remain eligible for **eight months after you enter or receive status,** unless your income increases above the allowable income for that program, or you fail to cooperate with the self-sufficiency plan that your case worker makes with you. If, for example, you apply for RCA two months after you are eligible, you will only get RCA for six months (the remaining period under the eight-month limit.)

How to Apply for RCA

Go to your local social services office to apply for RCA. Each state's social services office offers RCA. The name for this office is different in each state. You should be able to find where to go by searching on the Internet for the state you live in and "Refugee Cash Assistance." Take these things with you to the social services office:

- your I-94, Judge's Court Order, Asylum Office grant letter, or CP certification letter (for trafficking victim)
- your Social Security card
- proof of any income from your employer if employed
- proof of your address

If you do not yet have a Social Security card, bring proof that you have applied for it. To prove your address, bring an envelope addressed to you from a company or the U.S. government. If you are living with friends, bring a letter from your friends or the landlord stating that you live at that address. Some state social service offices also recommend bringing a letter from a Resettlement Agency stating your name, address, and need for assistance. They may ask for other things, but you can begin to apply with these.

The RCA eligibility process will take at least five days and may take several weeks. The social services office will assign you a caseworker. It may be the person who takes your application. If you do not get a letter within 10 days, call your caseworker.

Tip: Make sure to write down your caseworker's name and phone number before you leave the office. It is very important to tell your caseworker immediately if you move or get a job.

Supplemental Security Income (SSI)

What is SSI?

SSI is a U.S. government program that provides monthly stipends to low-income people who are blind, disabled, or age 65 or older. If you are not blind, disabled, or 65 or older, you cannot receive SSI.

SSI also is a "federally specified" program, which means it is run by the federal government (even though you must apply through a state agency) and the rules about who is eligible are the same in each state.

Who Is Eligible?

The SSI rules for immigrants are very restrictive. Only some of the "qualified immigrants" (listed above) are eligible to receive SSI *if* they meet one of the following conditions:

- Those who were lawfully residing in the U.S. on August 22, 1996 and now have a disability, or

- Those who were receiving SSI on August 22, 1996, or
- LPRs who have credit for "forty qualifying quarters of work"* in the U.S., and have had LPR status for at least five years.

* (A "qualifying quarter of work" is a three-month period in which enough income is earned to qualify as a "Social Security quarter." The Social Security Administration determines this amount each year. The shortest amount of time in which one person could earn 40 quarters is 10 years. The actual amount of time could be less because the hours that an immigrant's spouse or minor immigrant's parents work may count.)

However, refugees, asylees, those granted withholding of removal under the INA, trafficking victims, SIV holders, Cuban-Haitians, and Amerasians are immediately eligible for SSI if they meet other program requirements, but can only use it for the first seven years after being granted this status. Qualified immigrant veterans, active duty military members, and military spouses or children are also immediately eligible, and there is no time limit on how long they can use SSI.

Note: Even though most LPRs would have to wait 10 years before becoming eligible for SSI, LPRs become eligible to naturalize (become a U.S. citizen) after five years of being in LPR status. If someone naturalizes, s/he will not have to wait, because he or she will become eligible to apply for SSI as a U.S. citizen.

You cannot receive SSI while participating in the Matching Grant Program. Generally, if you are eligible for Matching Grant, you should try to complete that first. Then, if you are still in need after Matching Grant ends, apply for SSI.

CHAPTER 18

How Long Can I Receive SSI?

You can receive SSI for up to seven years after you arrive in the country as a refugee (or receive your protective status if you are in another eligible status), unless you qualify for SSI through another immigrant eligibility pathway outlined above that does not have a seven-year time limit (such as having received SSI since August 22, 1996). Otherwise, your eligibility ends seven years after you arrive in the country, unless you become a U.S. citizen.

How Do I Apply for SSI?

To see if you qualify and to set up an appointment to apply, contact the Social Security Administration at 1-800-772-1213 or go online to www.ssa.gov. You can find your local Social Security office online at www.socialsecurity.gov/locator. SSI is a "specified federal program," meaning it is a federal program, and eligibility and guidelines are set by the federal government. Therefore even though you must apply through a Social Security agency within your state, it is the same across the country, and eligibility is *not* determined by states.

You may need the following types of documents:

- Social Security number (if you do not have one, you may receive one if the Social Security Administration decides you are eligible for SSI or eligible because of your status)
- Proof of age (see Chapter 7, "Case Status and Proof of Status," for documents you can use)
- Proof of citizenship (see Chapter 7 for documents you can use)
- Proof of income (paychecks if you work)
- Proof of resources (bank statements, deeds or tax statements if you own property, life or disability insurance policies, titles or registrations for cars or other vehicles you own)
- Proof of living arrangements (lease or rent receipt for your

apartment, deed or property tax bill, receipts or information on other household expenses such as utilities and food)

Note: When you apply for SSI, the social services caseworker or eligibility worker will give you a form that tells you what else you must do to receive the benefit, or what other documents you must submit. If you fail to submit this information within the amount of time they tell you (usually 10 days), your case could be closed. This applies to all federal programs administered through state social services.

Does My State Have Similar Program I May Be Eligible For?
Some states have programs that are similar to SSI, which you may be eligible for even if you are not eligible for SSI. For a list of these programs, see the update page for NILC's Guide to Immigrant Eligibility for Federal Programs at http://nilc.org/guideupdate.html, and click on Table 9: State-funded SSI Replacement Programs.

Important! SSI is one of the few federal programs (TANF and public housing are the others) that are required to report to the U.S. government applicants who are not lawfully present, which could lead to your deportation. The circumstances of this reporting are very narrow; the agency is not required to report if you are only seeking benefits for your family members (and not yourself.) The agency will know that you are unlawfully present only if you present a written document such as a final order of deportation to them. If you are not sure if you are lawfully present, consult with a lawyer or BIA accredited representative.

CHAPTER 18

The Food Stamp Program (SNAP)

What is the Supplemental Nutrition Assistance Program (SNAP)?
Most people still refer to SNAP as the Food Stamp Program. SNAP provides vouchers or coupons to low-income people (people who do not make a lot of money) that can be used to buy food.

Who is Eligible?
"Qualified immigrants" (listed above) may be eligible to receive food stamps. SNAP is one of the "federal means-tested" programs, which means that many "qualified immigrant" adults must wait at least five years to get food stamps. However, refugees, asylees, those granted withholding of removal under the INA, trafficking victims, SIV holders, Cuban-Haitians, Amerasians, qualified immigrant veterans, active duty military members, and military spouses or children are immediately eligible, provided they meet the other program requirements. SNAP is also "federally specified," which means it is run by the federal government (even though you must apply through a state agency) and is the same in every state.

If you are an LPR (green card holder) adult, you must have been in status for five years, OR have 40 qualifying quarters of work. However, if you are not in one of these categories, you may not have to wait five years if you meet any of the following conditions:

- Under 18 years old, or
- Disabled or blind and receiving benefits or assistance for this, or
- Were born before August 22, 1931 and were lawfully residing in the U.S. on August 22, 1996, or
- A member of a Hmong or Laotian tribe that aided the U.S.

military in Vietnam, or
- American Indian.

In a crisis, you can get emergency food stamps quickly. This is called "expedited food stamps." An example of a crisis is being homeless and without food. The parents of a U.S. citizen child can also apply to get SNAP for their U.S. citizen child.

How Long Can I Receive Food Stamps?
There is no special time limit on SNAP benefits specific to immigrants.

How to Apply for SNAP
Each state has its own application, so you will need to contact your local Food Stamp Office or social service office to request one. Like SSI, SNAP is a "specified federal program," meaning it is a federal program, and eligibility and guidelines are set by the federal government. Therefore, even though you must apply through a state agency, it is the same across the country and eligibility is *not* determined by states. To find your local Food Stamp Office call 1-800-221-5689 or go online to www.fns.usda.gov/snap/.

Note: When you apply, the social services caseworker or eligibility worker will give you a form that tells you what else you must do to receive the benefit, or what other documents you must submit. If you fail to submit this information within the amount of time they tell you (usually 10 days), your case could be closed. This applies to all federal programs administered through state social services.

Special Help for Families

Families with children and pregnant women are eligible for additional programs. The rules for these programs are different in each state.

Temporary Assistance for Needy Families (TANF)

What is TANF?
TANF provides cash assistance for low-income families with children who are in the U.S. It is similar to RCA, but RCA is for single childless people, and TANF is for adults who have minor children with them. It has a federal work participation requirement for eligibility.

Important! TANF is the federal term for the program, but because it is state-run, it will likely have a different name in your state. Check with the eligibility worker at the state agency or with your refugee case worker for the correct name. Check the National Immigration Law Center's guide for your state's program and eligibility at http://nilc.org/guide_tanf.html.

Who Is Eligible for TANF?
"Qualified immigrants" (listed above) are eligible to receive TANF. TANF is one of the "federal means-tested" programs, which means many "qualified immigrants" must wait five years to become eligible. However, refugees, asylees, those granted withholding of removal under the INA, trafficking victims, SIV holders, Cuban-Haitians, Amerasians, qualified immigrant veterans, active duty military members, and military spouses or children are immediately eligible, provided they meet other program requirements.

Since a child born in the U.S. is automatically a U.S. citizen, immigrant parents of a U.S. citizen child can also apply to get TANF for their child, even if they themselves are not eligible.

TANF is a "federally designated" program, which means it is funded by the federal government, with required contributions from states. Within some federal guidelines, **each state makes its own rules.** About half the states use their own money to provide TANF to qualified immigrants or a broader group of lawfully residing immigrants without a waiting period. (However, a few states do not provide TANF to some qualified immigrants, even after their first five years in the U.S.)

It is very important that you check with your state, even if you do not think you are eligible, because the rules may be different in your state. Check the National Immigration Law Center's guide on TANF eligibility at http://nilc.org/guide_tanf.html to see if you are eligible for your state's program.

Are There Requirements I Must Meet to Continue to Receive TANF?
Yes, TANF has a work participation activity requirement. This program has different rules in each state or local area. Be sure to find out the rule and what you must do or your benefits will be stopped due to "non-compliance" (not following the rules).

You may qualify to receive either TANF or RCA (Refugee Cash Assistance); you may not receive both at the same time. You also may not receive TANF while participating in Matching Grant. **Generally, if you are eligible for Matching Grant, you should complete that first, then apply for RCA (if you are single), or TANF (if you have minor children with you in the U.S.) if you still need assistance.**

How Long Can I Use TANF?
The time limits and the treatment of mixed status households in TANF varies by state. In many states, TANF can last for up to five

years. Depending on your state, it could be terminated before the time limit expires if your income goes above the highest allowed amount, if your children are no longer minors, or if you do not respond to requests to supply updated information on your income and assets.

How Do I Apply for TANF?
Contact your local state social services office to learn more. You can also find out more about the TANF program if you call 1-202-401-5139 or go online to www.acf.hhs.gov/programs/ofa/. If you do not meet the requirements for the program (work participation activities, etc.) your benefits may be stopped. If you believe your benefits were stopped wrongly, you have the right to appeal. The appeal process must be explained to you in a language you understand.

Important! TANF is one of the few federal programs (SSI and public housing are the others) that are required to report to the U.S. government applicants who are not lawfully present, which could lead to your deportation. The circumstances of this reporting are very narrow; the agency is not required to report if you are only seeking benefits for your family members (and not yourself.) The agency will know that you are unlawfully present only if you present a written document such as a final order of deportation to them. If you are not sure if you are lawfully present, consult with a lawyer or BIA accredited representative.

Additional Programs for Families

- Women, Infants, and Children (WIC) is a national program that provides food vouchers or coupons, health care referrals, and nutrition education for low-income pregnant women, mothers up to a year after having a child, and children under five years old. You may be eligible for WIC regardless of your immigration status. Call 1-800-WIC-WINS (1-800-942-9467) or go online to www.fns.usda.gov/wic/ to find the office nearest you.

- Early Head Start and Head Start are child care programs that focus on education, health, and social development. For more information, contact your local school or the Head Start Bureau online at www.acf.hhs.gov/programs/ohs or 1-202-205-8572.
- Free breakfast and lunch programs are offered by some schools for their students. These programs may serve children all year long. Contact your local public school for more information or ask about this when you enroll your children in school.
- Your state may offer additional programs. Contact your local social services office or Resettlement Agency.

INFORMATION ON BENEFITS AVAILABLE BY STATUS

Refugees and Aslyees

As a refugee or asylee, you are eligible for the following programs discussed above:

- Matching Grant Program for up to four–six months after your arrival as a refugee or approval as an asylee (however, not all resettlement agencies receive Matching Grant funds, and those that do may have a limited amount of slots)
- RCA (Refugee Cash Assistance) for up to eight months after your arrival or approval

- SSI (Supplemental Security Income) for up to seven years after your arrival or approval, or unless you fit within another immigrant eligibility category
- SNAP (Supplemental Nutrition Assistance Program, also known as food stamps)
- TANF (Temporary Assistance for Needy Families)
- Other special programs for families listed above

Remember, you may not receive public cash assistance such as RCA (Refugee Cash Assistance), SSI (Supplemental Security Income), or TANF (Temporary Assistance for Needy Families) while you participate in the Matching Grant Program. It is recommended that you complete the Matching Grant Program first. Then, if you are not working when Matching Grant ends or if you still need assistance, apply for SSI (if you are blind, disabled, or over 65), RCA (if you do not have children), or TANF (if you have a family).

However, you *are* eligible to receive SNAP (Supplemental Nutrition Assistance Program, or food stamps), CHIP (Children's Health Insurance Program), RMA (Refugee Medical Assistance) or other public or health benefits at the same time as you participate in Matching Grant.

Withholding of Removal

You are unfortunately not eligible for the Matching Grant Program or RCA (Refugee Cash Assistance) *unless* you were granted withholding of removal as a Cuban-Haitian entrant. Otherwise, you may be eligible for the following programs discussed above:

- SSI (Supplemental Security Income) for seven years after your arrival or approval, unless you qualify based on another

immigrant eligibility category
- SNAP (Supplemental Nutrition Assistance Program)
- TANF (Temporary Assistance for Needy Families)
- Other special programs for families listed above

Asylum Seekers, and those Granted Deferral of Removal Under CAT

Unfortunately, there are not many programs you are eligible for federally. **However, if you are pregnant or have an infant or young child, you may be eligible for WIC. You should always check with your state,** because your state may have programs for which you are eligible.

Additionally, you are always eligible for the following services, regardless of status:

- School breakfasts and lunches
- WIC (food & healthcare program for Women, Infants, and Children)
- Short-term noncash emergency disaster assistance
- Other in-kind services necessary to protect life/safety (as long as no income qualifications are required for eligibility), including:
    - Child/adult protective services
    - Federal programs that address weather emergencies & homelessness
    - Shelters for domestic violence victims, runaway children, and the homeless
    - Soup kitchens
    - Community food banks

- o Meals-On-Wheels
- o Medical, public health, & mental health services necessary to protect public safety
- o Violence and abuse prevention
- o Disability/substance abuse services necessary to protect life/safety
- o Programs that protect safety of children, workers, and community residents

CHAPTER 19

How to Access Health Care

Emergency Medical Care

If you ever have a life-threatening medical emergency, dial 911 on any phone. Tell your name and the address from which you are calling and describe the symptoms you are having. If necessary, an ambulance will take you to a hospital for treatment. Your immigration status does not matter. It also does not matter whether you can pay. You have a right to get treatment for emergencies. Some examples of an emergency are a life-threatening wound or giving birth.

Everyone, regardless of immigration status (even undocumented immigrants) may be eligible to receive

- Federally-funded state medical assistance for emergency care, which includes emergency Medicaid, emergency room care, and labor and delivery;
- Short-term, non-cash, in-kind disaster relief;
- Public health assistance for immunizations and testing and

treatment for communicable diseases; and

- Assistance from programs that deliver in-kind services to the community (donations), do not make the donation dependent on your income or resources, and are necessary for your protection or safety (like soup kitchens, short-term shelters, and crisis counseling or intervention).

General Medical Care

Several programs provide financial support to certain immigrants to visit a doctor and get medicine. You can apply for these programs through your state social services office. The two main programs are Refugee Medical Assistance (RMA) and Medicaid.

Additionally, if you are a refugee or asylee, you must receive a medical examination with a doctor when you are admitted as a refugee or granted asylee status. This is a good time to ask any questions about any health concerns you may have, and ask how to treat medical problems you are experiencing.

Refugee Medical Assistance (RMA)

Refugee Medical Assistance (RMA) helps individuals or childless couples with low income or no income. RMA covers healthcare expenses for low-income refugees, asylees, parolees, Cuban-Haitian entrants, Amerasians, trafficking victims, and SIV holders. You become eligible for RMA as soon as you arrive as a refugee, parolee, Cuban-Haitian, or Amerasian; when you are granted asylum; when get your SIV; or when you are certified as a trafficking victim. You remain eligible for **eight months,** unless your income is above the allowable income for that program or you fail to cooperate with the self-sufficiency plan that your case worker makes with you. When these eight months are up, you can then apply for Medicaid.

HOW TO ACCESS HEALTH CARE

Medicaid

Medicaid is a program that helps pay for your healthcare costs if you are low-income (if you do not make a lot of money) and are of working age.

"Qualified immigrants" (listed in Chapter 18) are eligible to receive Medicaid. Medicaid is one of the "federal means-tested" programs, which means many "qualified immigrants" must wait five years to get Medicaid. However, refugees, asylees, those granted withholding of removal under the INA, trafficking victims, SIV holders, Cuban-Haitians, Amerasians, or qualified immigrant veterans, active duty military members, or military spouses or children are immediately eligible.

Medicaid is a "federally designated" program, which means it is funded by the federal government, with contributions from the states. Within federal guidelines, state rules may vary. About half the states use their own money to provide Medicaid to children and/or pregnant women who are either qualified immigrants or lawfully residing in the U.S. without a waiting period. A few states provide medical assistance to additional groups of immigrants who are ineligible for federal Medicaid, using their own funds. Therefore, it is very important that you check with your state, even if you do not think you are eligible, because the rules may be different in your state.

You may be eligible to use Medicaid for up to **seven years** after you arrive or are approved under your qualifying status, or until your income exceeds the income ceiling.

How to Apply

You can always see a doctor. However, health care in the U.S. can be expensive without insurance or a program like RMA. Health care in the U.S. is managed through large, private insurance companies. Go to your local social services office to apply for RMA or Medicaid. The name for this office is different in each state.

When you apply for Medicaid or RMA, the form will ask you to choose a company. If you already know which doctor you want to see, ask that doctor what insurance she or he accepts, then decide if that insurance is the one you want to select. You may also want to find out which health insurance companies will pay for interpreters when you go to medical appointments. Once you have been approved for Medicaid or RMA, you will receive a Medicaid card in the mail. This card is proof that Medicaid or RMA will pay your medical expenses. You may also need to get a medical card from your insurance company to show to the doctor or pharmacist when you need medical care, so they can bill your insurance company.

Doctors who accept Medicaid are required to provide an interpreter if you need one. It is never good to use a child as an interpreter in a medical situation. If you have an adult friend who is bilingual in English and your native language, it would be good for them to go with you. If you do not have someone to interpret for you, or if you do not want to talk about your medical issues in front of someone you know, you should tell the doctor's office that you will need an interpreter. The interpretation is usually done over the phone. If an interpreter is not available and you feel uncomfortable without an interpreter, ask to reschedule the appointment. Many doctors are unable to provide interpretation services. You may want to ask if your doctor or any staff are able to speak your language. If not, check with community groups or ethnic organizations who may offer interpretation services.

HOW TO ACCESS HEALTH CARE

Medicare

Medicare is a health insurance program for people who are age 65 or older or who have certain disabilities. If you meet these criteria, you may qualify for Part A "Premium Free," which covers the cost of inpatient care while you are in the hospital. Medicare Part A is available to some statuses, but the rules are very complex, and depend on how much U.S. work experience you have, among other criteria. Ask your state social services provider, case manager, or lawyer for help.

Part B "Buy in" Medicare has qualifying criteria similar to Part A. However, you are only eligible if you are an LPR (green card holder) and you have been in this status for at least five years. Part B Medicare covers doctors' services and outpatient hospital care.

If you are low-income, your state may help you pay for Part A and/or Part B. For more information, go online to www.socialsecurity.gov or call the Social Security Administration at 1-800-772-1213. You can also make an appointment with your local Social Security office. Go online to www.socialsecurity.gov/locator. For more information on Medicare, go online to www.medicare.gov.

CHIP (Children's Health Insurance Program)

What is CHIP?

CHIP provides free or low-cost health coverage to children up to age 19 whose family income is too high to qualify for Medicaid. Similarly to TANF, CHIP is administered by each state differently. All states cover regular check-ups, immunizations, hospital care, dental care, and lab and x-ray services. Preventive care (like check-ups) is often free, but other services may cost some money. Some states provide more than others, and some states provide CHIP through their Medicaid program.

CHAPTER 19

Who Is Eligible for CHIP?
"Qualified immigrants" (listed above) may be eligible to receive CHIP. CHIP is one of the "federal means-tested" programs, which means many "qualified immigrants" must wait at least five years to become eligible. However, refugees, asylees, those granted withholding of removal under the INA, trafficking victims, SIV holders, Cuban-Haitians, Amerasians, qualified immigrant veterans, active duty military members, and military spouses or children are immediately eligible, provided they meet the other CHIP program requirements. Parents can apply to get CHIP for their child, even if they themselves are not in any qualified status.

CHIP is a "federally designated program," which means it is funded in part by the federal government, but given to the states to administer, so each state makes its own rules, within federal guidelines. Under a federal option, about half the states use their own money to provide CHIP to qualified immigrants, as well as a broader group of lawfully residing children, without a waiting period. Additionally, about 15 states take advantage of another federal option in the CHIP program to provide prenatal care regardless of the mother's immigration status. Therefore, it is very important that you check with your state, even if you do not think you are eligible, because the rules may be different in your state.

How Do I Apply for CHIP?
To learn more about CHIP, you can either call 1-877-KIDS-NOW (1-877-543-7669), or visit http://insurekidsnow.gov/state/index.html and click on your state. Each state may have slightly different requirements.

New Options for Health Insurance from the Marketplace: The Patient Protection and Affordable Care Act (ACA)
Congress passed a law in 2010 called the Affordable Care Act, also known as "Obamacare," that should improve access to healthcare

for many immigrants. Many parts of the law went into effect in January 2014. Among other things, the ACA created new health insurance "Marketplaces" or "exchanges." These exchanges provide a new way for you to find health insurance that fits your health and budgetary needs. The plans on the exchanges are owned by private insurance companies, and you can compare the plans side by side. No one can turn you down for illnesses or medical conditions you have.

Individuals who are "lawfully present" are eligible to apply for new affordable coverage options as of January 1, 2014, and to enroll in state or federally-run health insurance exchanges. Lawfully present individuals will also be able to apply for premium tax credits to pay for plans purchased under the exchanges. Some non-pregnant adults, including some immigrants, will become eligible for their state's Medicaid program.

Those "Lawfully Present" and Eligible for Healthcare Under the ACA ("Obamacare"):

- Refugees
- Asylees
- Withholding of Removal *(under the INA and CAT)*
- LPRs (lawful permanent residents, or green card holders), *and applicants for adjustment of status to LPR*
- *Asylum Seekers and applicants for Withholding of Removal and protection under CAT who have employment authorization and have had their applications pending for 180 days*
- Conditional entrants (what refugees were called before 1980)
- Parolees of at least one year
- Cuban and Haitian entrants
- Certain battered (abused) immigrants and their children and/or spouses (VAWA self-petitioners)
- Trafficking victims

- SIV (Special Immigrant Visas for Iraqis and Afghans) recipients
- Temporary Protected Status (TPS), *and TPS applicants* who have employment authorization
- Deferred Enforced Departure
- Deferred Action (unfortunately not including those granted Deferred Action for Childhood Arrivals, or DACA)
- Special Immigrant Juvenile Status (SIJS) recipients *and applicants*
- U-visa holders (immigrant victims of crimes)
- Final orders of removal released under order of supervision who have an employment authorization document (EAD) *(this includes Deferral Under CAT)*
- Applicants for cancellation of removal or suspension of deportation
- Lawful temporary residents
- SAW applicants under IRCA
- LIFE Act immigrants with employment authorization
- Family Unity (spouses and children of noncitizens who legalized under IRCA)
- Registry applicants
- Non-Immigrant Status (worker visas, student visas, citizens of Micronesia, Marshall Islands, and Palau)
- Members of federally recognized Indian tribes, American Indians born in Canada, and residents of Samoa

Those NOT Lawfully Present

ACA does not include undocumented immigrants or those granted DACA relief. Noncitizens in these categories will not be able to participate in the federal or state exchanges, receive tax subsidies, or enroll in federal nonemergency Medicaid. They will not be required to purchase health insurance. Of course, they can purchase full-priced healthcare plans outside the exchanges.

HOW TO ACCESS HEALTH CARE

How to Apply

You will need to fill out a single application for the Marketplace, and there are many resources available to help you. You can access the Marketplace at www.healthcare.gov, or by calling 1-800-318-2596. You may also send a paper application in the mail to:

Health Insurance Marketplace
Department of Health and Human Services
465 Industrial Blvd.
London, KY 40750

It is recommended that you get someone to help you review the plans available to you, decide which plans fit your needs best, and apply. You can find out whether your state uses its own Marketplace or the federal Marketplace, and where to apply in your state at www.healthcare.gov/what-is-the-marketplace-in-my-state. You can find help from a Marketplace "Navigator," or someone whose job it is to help you understand the Marketplace, by filling in where you live at https://localhelp.healthcare.gov.

Important! The application for Marketplace insurance now appears in over 30 languages common to the refugee population in the U.S. at this website: http://marketplace.cms.gov/applications-and-forms/individuals-and-families-forms.html.

Applicants for health coverage under Medicaid, CHIP, or the health insurance Marketplace will need to provide information about their immigration status and Social Security number. Individuals who are applying for coverage for their family members, but are not seeking coverage for themselves, do not need to provide this information about themselves. The information will be used only to determine eligibility for health coverage, and **ICE has clarified**

that any information provided will not be used for immigration enforcement purposes.

The following documentation may be required for ACA coverage, depending on your status:

- Permanent Resident Card, "Green Card" (I-551) (for LPRs)
- Reentry Permit (I-327)
- Refugee Travel Document (I-571)
- Employment Authorization Card (I-766) (work permit)
- Machine Readable Immigrant Visa (with temporary I-551 language)
- Temporary I-551 Stamp (on passport or I-94/I-94A)
- Arrival/Departure Record (I-94/I-94A)
- Arrival/Departure Record in foreign passport (I-94)
- Foreign passport
- Certificate of Eligibility for Nonimmigrant Student Status (I-20)
- Certificate of Eligibility for Exchange Visitor Status (DS2019)
- Notice of Action (I-797)
- Document indicating membership in a federally recognized Indian tribe or American Indian born in Canada
- Certification from U.S. Department of Health and Human Services (HHS) Office of Refugee Resettlement (ORR)
- Office of Refugee Resettlement (ORR) eligibility letter (if under 18)
- Document indicating withholding of removal
- Alien number or 1-94 number

Individuals who do not have these documents may be able to offer other proof of their status (such as a court order).

In order to learn more about the Affordable Care Act, how to sign up, and what it means for you and your family, please see www.

healthcare.gov/immigration-status-and-the-marketplace/.

Additional Tips

If you do not have insurance and you have a medical emergency, your caseworker can help you. Many hospitals have programs that allow people to pay only what they can. Each state has a Refugee Health Coordinator who would know what health programs and services are available in your local area. You can find your state's Refugee Health Coordinator by calling the Office of Refugee Resettlement at 202-401-9246 or by going online to www.acf.hhs.gov/programs/orr/resource/orr-funded-programs-key-contacts.

Additionally, the Refugee Health Information Network and the U.S. Committee for Refugees and Immigrants have a lot of information about health care, hygiene, and physical and mental health, including the "Healthy Living Toolkit." This information about health can be found in many languages online at www.refugees.org/resources/for-refugees--immigrants/health/. Additionally, ORR (Office of Refugee Resettlement) has helpful resources on the Marketplace and health insurance generally at www.acf.hhs.gov/programs/orr/health.

You can find more information on mental health in Chapter 23, "How to Get Emotional Support."

Federally Qualified Health Centers

Federally qualified health centers provide medical care to individuals regardless of their immigration status. They are more able than doctors to arrange for interpreters. These health centers often work on a sliding scale—that means you pay only what you are able.

Go online to www.bphc.hrsa.gov to find a federally qualified health center. Type in your zip code in the "Find a Health Center" box in the upper righthand corner.

Dental Care

Dental care is care for your teeth. Often schools where students are studying to be dentists will offer affordable or even free dental work. Look in the phone book or online for listings of area universities and colleges that have dental schools or free/low cost dental clinics.

Important! Some people think that it is okay to ignore dental problems or not have regular dental check-ups. However, problems with your teeth can cause many other dangerous health problems, including heart disease. Be sure to make regular dental appointments and see a dentist if you have problems with your teeth!

Getting Prescriptions

Some drug stores and discount stores may have their own "generic" low-priced form of some prescriptions you need.

How Do I Get My Medical Records from the Detention Facility?

Did you see a doctor while you were in detention? If so, you have the right to get a copy of your medical records. Call the detention center and ask how to get a copy. Or ask a resettlement agency to send a release form to the center. For more information, see Chapter 6, "How to Get Your Personal Property After You Are Released From Detention."

HOW TO ACCESS HEALTH CARE

INFORMATION ON HEALTH INSURANCE BY STATUS

Refugees & Asylees

If you are single or have children with you in the U.S., you have access to Refugee Medical Assistance (RMA), which pays healthcare expenses for low-income refugees and asylees for up to eight months after you arrive or are granted asylum. You should apply for RMA as soon as you arrive or are granted status, as it only covers you for eight months after you become eligible, not for eight months after you apply. Once your RMA expires, you may be eligible for Medicaid, which pays healthcare expenses for low-income people of working age, depending on income requirements of your state. However, you cannot use both at the same time. Your children 19 and under are eligible for CHIP (Children's Health Insurance Program) if you meet the other program qualifications.

If you have sufficient work history in the U.S. and are a senior or a person with disabilities, you may also be eligible for Medicare, a program that helps pay for the medical expenses of people over the age of 65 and people of any age with disabilities and certain diseases. You are considered "lawfully present," and are eligible for affordable health care options under the Affordable Care Act. You should visit : www.acf.hhs.gov/programs/orr/health and watch the informative video on refugees and the Affordable Care Act, available in six different languages.

Asylum Seekers

You are eligible for fewer programs than refugees and asylees, but you do have options. You are considered "lawfully present" if you have work authorization, which makes you eligible to apply for affordable health care options in a federal or state-run exchange under the Affordable Care Act. If you have sufficient work history in the U.S., you may be eligible for Medicare Part A if you are over the age of 65, or are any age and have disabilities or certain diseases. You are eligible for immunizations and treatment of communicable diseases. You can always be treated in an emergency, and are eligible for emergency medical coverage, such as emergency Medicaid, emergency room services, labor and delivery, and other services listed at the beginning of this chapter under "Emergency Medical Care." In some states, children and pregnant women may be eligible for Medicaid.

Withholding of Removal Under the INA

You may be eligible for Medicaid. You are considered "lawfully present," which makes you eligible to apply for affordable health care options in a federal or state-run exchange under the Affordable Care Act. If you have sufficient work history, you may be eligible for Medicare Part A if you are over the age of 65, or are any age and have disabilities or certain diseases. You are eligible for Medicaid, and your children are eligible for CHIP, if you meet the other program qualifications. You can always be treated in an emergency, and may be eligible for emergency medical coverage, such as emergency Medicaid, emergency room services, labor and delivery, and other services listed at the beginning of this chapter under "Emergency Medical Care."

Withholding of Removal Under CAT

You are considered "lawfully present," which makes you eligible to apply for affordable health care options in a federal or state-run exchange under the Affordable Care Act. If you have sufficient work history, you may be eligible for Medicare Part A if you have work authorization and are over the age of 65, or have work authorization and are any age and have disabilities or certain diseases. You can always be treated in an emergency, and may be eligible for emergency medical coverage, such as emergency Medicaid, emergency room services, labor and delivery, and other services listed at the beginning of this chapter under "Emergency Medical Care."

Deferral Under CAT

You are considered "lawfully present" if you are released under an order of supervision, and have work authorization on that basis, which makes you eligible to apply for affordable health care options in a federal or state-run exchange under the Affordable Care Act. You can always be treated in an emergency, and may be eligible for emergency medical coverage, such as emergency Medicaid, emergency room services, labor and delivery, and other services listed at the beginning of this chapter under "Emergency Medical Care."

CHAPTER 20

How to Access Housing

When you first arrive in the U.S., finding a place to live can be difficult. However, there are many housing options for individuals of all income levels and immigration statuses.

Temporary Housing

If you suddenly find yourself without a place to live or at risk of losing your shelter, most large cities have temporary homeless shelters. Homeless shelters that receive federal money are required to let people stay there, regardless of their immigration status. Every shelter has individual policies on how long you are allowed to stay. Please visit www.homelessshelterdirectory.org/ for a list of homeless shelters in your state.

Many people stay with family or friends until they are able to find a place of their own. If you are far from family and friends, home-sharing programs or communal living are possible temporary housing options. Home-sharing and communal living opportunities involve paying to live with someone in their home, or paying to live in a shared space with several others. The National Shared Housing Resource Center has a directory of home-sharing programs that can be found online at www.nationalsharedhousing.org. The Fellowship for Intentional Communities also has a directory of community living opportunities online at www.fic.ic.org.

Additionally, religious groups, such as churches, temples, and mosques, sometimes help to find and pay for housing for a short period of time.

If you or your children are the victim of abuse by your partner or spouse and you are afraid to stay in your home, you should call the National Domestic Violence Hotline at 1-800-799-7233 or 1-800-787-3224 or go online to www.thehotline.org. They can offer you support in 170 languages and refer you to domestic violence shelters.

Long-term Housing

When you are financially stable, renting an apartment is one possible housing option. Renting an apartment involves paying a landlord (or the owner of the building) a monthly fee (rent) for a small living space. An apartment typically includes a kitchen, living room, bathroom, and bedroom(s). Look in your local newspaper, or visit www.craigslist.org to find available apartments in your community.

Housing in the U.S. can be very expensive. You may want to look into renting an efficiency or studio (an apartment with one room for sleeping and living) instead of a one-bedroom. Living with roommates is also usually cheaper than living alone.

Prior to moving in, you will have to sign a lease. A lease is a formal agreement between the landlord and you (the renter), outlining the expectations and responsibilities of each person. The lease will specify the amount of your monthly rent and the date you must pay it by. It will state the number of people allowed to live in the apartment, how many days' notice you must give before moving out, and the responsibilities of the landlord. Make sure you ask if utilities (gas, electricity, and water) are included in the rent, or if you must pay for those separately. Lastly, you may be required to put down a security deposit. A security deposit is a sum of money that you give the landlord before moving in. You will receive the money back when you move out, if the apartment has not been damaged.

Public or Assisted Housing

Depending on where you live, rent can be very expensive. If your annual income is low, you may be eligible for government funded public or subsidized housing. Public housing programs provide safe and affordable rental housing for eligible low-income families, the elderly, and persons with disabilities. The monthly price you pay is dependent on your financial situation. Most families pay 30% of their monthly adjusted income. To receive the benefits, all participants are required to live in housing located in subsidized housing projects. For more information on specific public housing programs, or to learn how to apply, please visit http://portal.hud.gov/hudportal/HUD?src=/topics/rental_assistance/phprog.

Subsidized housing, or the Housing Choice Vouchers Program, allows very low-income families, the elderly, and persons with disabilities to choose and lease or purchase safe, decent and affordable privately-owned rental housing. You are free to live in any house or apartment that meets the requirements of the program, and are not limited to those located in subsidized housing projects. If you qualify for the program, you will be issued a housing voucher. You are then responsible for finding housing where the landlord, or owner, agrees to participate in the program. Every month, through your voucher, the government will pay a portion of your rent. Your family is responsible for paying the remaining amount. For more information on specific subsidized housing programs, or to learn how to apply, please visit http://portal.hud.gov/hudportal/HUD?src=/program_offices/public_indian_housing/programs/hcv/about.

All listed programs are available for lawful permanent residents, refugees, asylees, parolees, conditional entrants, Cuban and Haitian entrants, certain battered immigrants, certain people with a T-visa (for trafficking victims) or U-visa (immigrant victims of crimes), or families with at least one person who has a Social Security number and is eligible to work in the U.S. Someone at your local resettlement agency or state social services office can help you learn more about your options. There is usually a long wait for subsidized housing—sometimes several years. Priority is given to families with children.

Important! Public housing is one of the few federal programs (TANF and SSI are the others) that are required to report to the U.S. government applicants who are not lawfully present, which could result in your deportation. The circumstances of this reporting are very narrow; the agency is not required to report if you are only seeking benefits for your family members (and not yourself.) The agency will know that you are unlawfully present only if you present a written document such as a final order of deportation to them. If you are not sure if you are lawfully present, consult with a lawyer or BIA accredited representative.

If you are in the Matching Grant Program and need housing, your caseworker will help you. The Matching Grant Program also helps to pay rent for the first four months after you are deemed eligible.

For more information on Matching Grant, see Chapter 18, "How to Get Public Benefits and Financial Support."

CHAPTER 21

How to Access Education and Childcare

There are many valuable opportunities in the U.S. for you and your children to pursue an education.

Childcare Options for Young Children

For families where the primary caretaker works full-time, there are a variety of daytime childcare options for children ages one to four. If family or friends are not available, you can send your child to daycare or preschool. At daycare, a trained individual cares for your child in their home or at a daycare center while the parent is at work. Preschool is a more formal program, where a certified teacher offers daily lessons in a classroom setting, to better prepare your child for school. The cost and availability of both programs varies greatly. Look online or in the phone book to locate a program in your area.

Your family might also be eligible for participation in Head Start. If family or friends are not available to care for your children while you work, Head Start is a federal program that helps to prepare children from approximately age three to five for school. Eligibility is based on financial need, not immigration status. While eligibility requirements may vary regionally, generally to qualify your family's income must be at or below the federal poverty line, your family must be faced with homelessness, your family must be receiving TANF or SSI, or the child must be in foster care. To learn more about Head Start, please visit http://eclkc.ohs.acf.hhs.gov/hslc/hs/about. To locate a Head Start program close to you, please visit http://eclkc.ohs.acf.hhs.gov/hslc/HeadStartOffices or call 1-866-763-6481.

Important! In the U.S., leaving your children at home alone is often considered neglect, a form of child abuse. **If you leave your child at home alone, the government may take your child away from you.** The laws are different in each state, but you generally should not leave a child under 12 home alone. You should check with your state's child welfare agency to find out the requirements in your state: www.childwelfare.gov/pubs/reslist/rl_dsp_website.cfm?rs_ID=16&rate_chno=AZ-0004E.

Most states also issue childcare vouchers, which you can apply for through your state social services agency as long as you are employed.

Primary and Secondary Education for Children Ages 5 to 18:
In the U.S., every child, regardless of their immigration status, has the right to a free public education from kindergarten through grade 12. If you are the parent or guardian of a child under the age of 18, by law you are required to send them to school. Some states require school attendance only through age 16. Visit your state's Board of Education website for more information. You are also required to make sure your child goes to school on time and every day unless they are sick or there is an emergency. If your child will not be at school, you must call the school to let them know why your child will be absent. For more information on how to enroll your child in school, visit

your home state's Board of Education website or speak with your caseworker or sponsor. At the time of registration, most schools require proof of residency (a copy of a phone bill, a water bill, or a lease agreement is acceptable), and a copy of your child's birth certificate, or other proof of your child's date of birth. The birth certificate will only be used to confirm your child's age. **A school cannot require you to share proof of immigration status or a Social Security number.** Additionally, many schools require that all children have medical examinations and immunizations before they start school. When you register your child for school, ask what immunizations are required and whether the local health department offers them free of charge.

Children usually start school when they are four or five years old and graduate when they are 17 or 18 years old. However, some school districts will allow students to stay in school until they graduate or turn 21. Visit your state's Board of Education website for more information. This schooling includes primary/elementary school, middle school, and high school. Most children go to public schools, which are free and open to all. Some parents pay for their children to go to private school.

Many schools also have after-school programs to help with homework, and counselors who can talk to children if they are having a hard time at school. U.S. schools expect parents to be actively involved in their child's education. This includes reminding your child to do his/her homework, contacting the teacher if you have a concern about your child, and attending parent-teacher conferences.

Many schools offer free or low cost breakfast, lunch, and milk to eligible students. Eligibility is based on financial need, and is not determined by immigration status. Students are eligible if they are members of a household that receives SNAP or TANF benefits; if they are categorized as homeless, migrants, or runaways as defined by law; or if they are enrolled in a Head Start or Even Start program. Ask for more information when you register your child for school.

Any student who lives farther than 1.5 miles (distance varies depending on the school district) from the nearest public school is eligible to ride the school bus. The school bus will pick students up before school and drop them off after school at a designated stop every day. When you register your child for school, ask if there is a fee to ride the bus, and if financial assistance is available.

If your child has a documented disability, or if you believe he or she might have a physical or mental disability, it is important to notify the school. Schools are required to provide additional, individualized support to all children with disabilities through age 21. Upon your notifying the school of a disability, they are required to conduct a free evaluation to determine if your child is eligible for special education services. If your child does have a disability, the school is required to work with you and their teachers to develop an Individualized Educational Program (IEP) specific to their needs.

If English is not your child's first language, the school is required to conduct a language evaluation to determine if your child is eligible for English as a Second Language (ESL) classes. ESL classes provide additional one-on-one or small group English language instruction. Speak with your school administrators or counselors about enrolling your child in ESL classes.

Upon completing and passing grade 12, a student graduates from high school, and receives a high school diploma. A high school diploma is an important achievement. Many jobs in the U.S. require applicants to have a high school diploma, or to have passed the General Educational Development (GED) exam. The GED is a series of five exams in science, mathematics, social studies, reading, and writing. As soon as an individual passes, they have a credential equivalent to a high school diploma. A GED is recognized and honored in all 50 states. The exam must be taken at an official GED Testing Center. For more information about the exam, or to locate a testing center, please visit: www.gedtestingservice.com/ged-testing-service.

Higher Education

Higher education is the voluntary (your choice) schooling that happens after completion of the required elementary, middle, and high school education. Higher education can take many different forms, including community college, technical and vocational college, liberal arts college, or university. For more information on higher educational opportunities, as well as the enrollment process, please visit www.collegeboard.org/.

There is currently no federal or state law preventing undocumented immigrants or noncitizens from attending public or private institutions of higher education. However, individual school policies differ greatly. Contact the admissions office at a specific school for more information. Many states have passed legislation allowing in-state tuition, which is often lower than out-of-state tuition (the price of school for students from a different state than that of the school) for undocumented immigrants in public universities. Check with National Immigration Forum at www.immigrationforum.org or the National Immigration Law Center at www.nilc.org.

Higher education can be very expensive. Scholarships can help to offset the cost. A scholarship is money given by national and community organizations, religious groups, the government, or the school itself to help pay for educational costs. Some private scholarships may require recipients to be U.S. citizens or legal residents.

You are eligible for student financial aid from the U.S. Department of Education if you are a permanent resident, U.S. national, refugee, asylee, Cuban-Haitian entrant, conditional entrant, parolee, battered immigrant (VAWA), trafficking victim, or SIV holder. Financial aid includes work study programs, the Pell grant, and certain government loans such as Stafford and Perkins loans. Citizens of the Federated States of Micronesia, the Republic of the Marshall Islands, or the Republic of Palau are eligible for Federal Pell Grants, Federal Supplemental Educational Opportunity Grants, and Federal Work Study. To learn more visit www.studentaid.ed.gov or www.fafsa.ed.gov.

For more information about educational opportunities, you can call one of these numbers:

- Federal Student Aid Information Center: 1-800-433-3243
- U.S. Department of Education: 1-800-USA-LEARN (1-800-872-5327)
- Your local resettlement agency (see Chapter 25, "Directory of Resettlement Agencies [RAs]")

Adult Education

Many local community colleges, churches, non-profits, and community centers offer free and/or reduced cost adult or community education classes. These classes are open to anyone, and are a great way to meet members of your community and to learn a new skill. Possible courses often include English language instruction, foreign language classes, fitness and nutrition, computer literacy, art classes, cooking classes, and home repair. Look online or in the phone book to locate programs offered in your area.

SECTION 4

Integration, Interpersonal Connections, and Community Support

CHAPTER 22

How to Keep Your Money Safe and Make it Grow

Banking in the United States

In the U.S., many people use banks to help them with their money. There are many reasons to use a bank. Your money will be safe from being stolen or lost. Using a bank costs less than using a check cashing store. If you have a bank account and you work, having your employer directly deposit your paycheck into your bank account is free and safer than receiving paper checks. If you put money in a Savings Account, you can earn interest (extra money) for your future. You may want to open both a checking and a savings account.

Checking Accounts

A checking account is what most Americans have for daily use. It is called a checking account because when you write a check, the money will come out of this account. You also can deposit checks from your job or from other people into this account. Check cashing stores often charge a fee, but if you have a bank account, you will be able to cash your checks free of charge there. (To "cash a check" means to take a check to a bank or check cashing store and exchange the check for money, which comes out of the bank account of the person giving you the check.) When you open an account, you will be given a supply of checks, which are paper forms that tell the bank to pay money from the check writer's account.

You will also be given an ATM card (also called a "debit card") for bank transactions. It is a small plastic card that you can use to pay for things, and the money will come directly out of your account. You can withdraw spending money by using this card at an automated teller machine (ATM) or going to the bank. The bank will ask you to create a personal identification number (PIN) to use when taking money out or paying for something. It is your secret password that you should not give to anyone, because they could use it to take money from your account.

If you write a check, withdraw money, or pay for things with your ATM card, you must make sure you have enough money in your account—otherwise, you will have to pay a penalty.

When you get a job, you will begin receiving paychecks. You have several choices related to your pay:

- Get cash for your check at a check-cashing store. There may be a large fee for this.
- Receive a paper check and deposit it into your bank account.
- Ask your employer for "direct deposit."

Direct deposit is the safest, fastest, and most convenient way to get paid. You give your employer your bank account information, and your employer then electronically transfers each paycheck into your bank account, instead of giving you a paper check to cash or deposit yourself. If you do not arrange for direct deposit and instead take your checks to the bank yourself, you will often experience a delay of a few days before the money is available. If you arrange for direct deposit, your money is immediately available when your employer completes the transfer.

Tip: If you get a job, ask your employer for direct deposit. Your employer will not have the power to take money out of your bank account; they will only have the power to put money into your account.

Savings Accounts

Most Americans also have savings accounts. You can put money into and take money out of most savings accounts in the same way as you do with checking accounts. But while your checking account is generally for making purchases, paying bills, and writing checks, your savings account is a place for you to put money away for the future. While the money stays in the savings account, it gathers interest.

Interest is a percentage of money the bank pays, based on how much money you have in your account on average each month. The more money you have in your savings account, the more money it will gather in interest. Many savings accounts have a 0.05% interest rate. So if you have an average of $100 in your savings account, you will gather 5 cents per month in interest. If you have $1,000, it will gather 50 cents. If you have $10,000, it will gather $5, etc.

Many Americans put a certain percentage of each paycheck into a savings account and leave it there to gather interest for years, only taking it out for emergencies, large events such as weddings, or when they are old and stop working. The longer you leave money in your account, the more it will accumulate.

Tip: Ask your resettlement agency for classes or tips on how to manage your money, including how much money to budget for each month and how much to put into savings.

Individual Development Account

You may be able to start saving before you think it is possible. In some areas of the country, the Office of Refugee Resettlement offers the Individual Development Account (IDA) program for asylees, refugees, and trafficking victims. The program is often jointly run by a resettlement agency and a bank. An IDA can help you save money. If you are low-income and have little savings, you may be eligible for IDA. If you have IDA, the government may match the money you save. If you save $1, the government will give you $1. If you save $100, the government will give you $100. The government will match your savings up to $2000 per person or $4000 per household. The money you save must be for education, a house, or other important items such as a car. The government match money is not available to you until you have saved the full amount that you chose as your goal when you entered the program. Note that if you do not meet your goal, the government will not match the funds.

People with IDA also receive basic training on how to save, build credit, and understand the U.S. financial system. Your local resettlement agencies and social services office can help you learn more about this money saving option. You can also learn more about it online at www.acf.hhs.gov/programs/orr/programs/ida/about.

Opening a Bank Account

You can open a bank account by yourself, or open a joint account with your spouse or another person. Visit several banks in your area to see which has the best services to fit your needs. Some resettlement agencies have classes to help you learn how to manage your money. They can give you advice about getting bank accounts.

Each bank has a policy on what documents you need to get a new account. Usually you will need an identification card with your photo on it, a Social Security card (if you have one), and proof of your address, such as a utility bill or a pay stub. Ask the bank what documents they require, and then see Chapter 7 for tips on what documents you can use to show your status.

Electronic Banking

Electronic banking, or electronic funds transfer (EFT), is a way to pay for things or move money electronically. It can be confusing, because you do not see the money. Immigrants often pay very high fees for wire services to send money back to their families in their home countries. Banks often offer wire services to their customers at a much lower rate than regular wire services. If you plan to send money to family members in your home country, ask about wire service fees.

Credit Cards

Credit is a system that allows one person to borrow money from another person or financial institution. Credit cards are a convenient way to purchase items you want. Credit cards can be very helpful if you must make a large purchase, but do not have the money immediately available to pay for it. Instead, you pay a portion of the price each month, plus interest, until you pay off the debt.

For example, if you need to purchase a piece of furniture that costs $1,000, you may not have enough money for groceries and other expenses that month if you pay the entire $1,000 at once. Instead, if you pay for your furniture with a credit card, the credit card company will pay the furniture company, and will then send you a monthly bill for a part of the cost, say $75 per month. You will continue to pay each month until you pay it off the entire $1,000.

However, just as savings accounts gather interest, so do credit card balances, or the amount left to pay. This means that each month, the credit card company charges you a percentage of the total balance. The longer you take to pay off your balance, the more money you must spend. If you pay off your balance immediately, you do not have to pay interest. Therefore, it is wise to only use your credit card to pay for items you can pay off immediately unless it is absolutely necessary to carry a balance, and then pay that off as soon as you can.

Using credit cards responsibly can help you gain a good credit rating. Good credit will help when you want to pay for higher education or buy an expensive items such as a house. To get good credit, **it is very important to pay back the money on time.** If you apply to a bank or financial institution for a credit card, that company will check to find out if you have been paying your bills on time. If you have not been doing so, they have the right to deny you a credit card.

You may want to talk to a friend or someone at your local resettlement agency before you get a credit card. Credit cards can be helpful, but it is important that you understand the risks of getting a credit card. You may want to start with a credit card that has a low annual fee and low borrowing limit. If you have a $1,000 limit on your credit card, it will be easier for you to practice controlling your debt and pay it back in a reasonable amount of time.

HOW TO KEEP YOUR MONEY SAFE AND MAKE IT GROW

Budget

Many Americans make a budget, which is a plan for how much money you can spend in a given period of time, usually a month. It is based on your income (how much money you make from your job, cash assistance programs, or any other form of payment to you) and your needs.

Most Americans have these major living costs:

- Rent or mortgage (monthly payment on your apartment or house): This will probably be your largest expense each month.
- Childcare: In many American families, both parents work. Because many Americans do not live near their relatives, they need to hire someone to watch the children while they are at work. **Do not leave young children at home alone! This is considered unsafe in America, and the government could take your children away.** Childcare can be expensive. Ask your resettlement agency for tips on where to find affordable childcare, and see Chapter 21, "How to Access Education and Childcare."
- Transportation: Owning a car is very expensive. It will be cheaper to take buses, metros, or other public transportation if it is available where you live.
- Telephone: Most Americans have mobile (cell) phones, and many also have a landline (a phone in your home).
- Food: Food can be expensive, but you can keep costs down by cooking food like rice, beans, and vegetables at home. See Chapter 18 for programs you may be eligible for, such as SNAP (food stamps), or other financial benefits that may

give you access to more affordable food.

  - o **Tip:** There is a lot of "fast food," such as McDonald's and Burger King, available in the U.S. It is cheap and fast, and many people eat it often for those reasons. However, it is very unhealthy, and may cost you a lot more money in the long run because it can cause many serious health problems that will require a lot of expensive medical treatment. Cooking healthy food at home, avoiding sodas and other processed foods, and drinking a lot of water is cheaper and healthier. Ask your resettlement agency, community organization, or lawyer for resources on healthy eating and living.

- Utilities: Utilities are services such as electricity, oil, water, and trash collection that you need to live in your apartment or house. Some utilities might be included in your rent, most commonly water and trash collection. In most places, you must pay your own electricity and gas bills (for your stove and heat). Be careful, as your bills can become very high during the summer or winter months if you use more air conditioning or heat.

TIPS:

- Be sure to pay all your bills on time. If you do not, it could be more difficult to reach your future financial goals—goals such as buying a house or car.
- It is very important for refugees to pay what is due on travel loans every month on time. Not repaying loans on time will also ruin your credit.
- Some Americans find it easier to pay all their bills online, instead of sending in checks by mail every month. You can set up a payment schedule each month, and you don't have

to worry about mail getting lost or delayed. Ask your resettlement agency, community organization, or bank how to do this if you find it confusing.

- It is not safe to carry around a lot of money with you, or even to have a lot of money in your house, because it could be stolen or lost. It is best to keep most of your money in your bank accounts.
- Write down the numbers for all of your bank accounts, debit cards, ATM cards, and credit cards. Write down the phone numbers for each of these companies. **Keep this information in a safe place, and do not share it with others.** If your wallet, cards, or checkbook ever get lost or stolen, call the companies and have them cancel your accounts. This means no one will be able to use your cards illegally and take money from your accounts, and the bank or credit card companies will send you new cards. This is an important step to take to keep your money safe.
- Keep important documents from your home country, such as your passport, birth certificate, marriage certificate, and any documents or diplomas that show your education in a safe place, along with important personal or confidential documents from the U.S. such as your Social Security card.
- If you need to send any personal documents or checks in the mail, make sure you put them in a U.S. Postal Service blue collection box, give it to a mail carrier, or take it to a post office.

Avoiding Fraud and Scams

Websites

While many people in the U.S. will want to help you in your journey, some people will try to take advantage of you because you may be unfamiliar with the way things work in the U.S., and you may not yet speak or understand English as well as you will one day. Some dishonest people have created websites that look like government websites, or bank websites, to confuse you and take advantage of you. Until you are familiar with government websites, make sure you ask your resettlement agency, BIA accredited representative, or lawyer before using a website. Do not enter any of your personal information, such as your Social Security number or bank accounts, into unfamiliar websites.

Legal Services

Some people who say they are qualified to offer legal services are not. Some consultants, travel agencies, real estate offices, and people called "notaries public" offer immigration services. Be sure to ask questions about their qualifications and ask to see copies of their BIA accreditation letter or law certificate.

These people are dangerous because they often say they can file your asylum or other legal claim, take a lot of money from you, and then do not file your paperwork. This can cause major problems with your case, and in extreme circumstances, can cause you to lose your case. You can go online to www.uscis.gov/avoidscams for tips on how to avoid seeking help from people who are not experts. You can also check www.justice.gov/eoir/discipline.htm for a list of lawyers who have been disciplined by EOIR for bad practice of immigration law.

Emails and Phone Calls

Sometimes, dishonest people will send emails from fake email accounts that may look like they are from your bank, but are not. Never respond to an email that says it is from a bank needing your bank account information, PIN, or Social Security number—this is a scammer trying to take your money. Some people also pretend to be a bank, credit card company, or government agency, and call you on the phone, claiming to need your personal information, or claiming you owe the government money. This is a scam. Never give your Social Security number, PIN, bank account, or other important information over the phone, and do not send money to people you do not know.

Tips to Avoid Scams

- Keep your PIN secret.
- When creating your PIN, do not use numbers that are easy for other people to guess, such as "12345," your date of birth, or your address.
- Never write your PIN on your ATM or debit card.
- If your debit or credit card has been lost, contact your bank immediately.
- Make sure you get a receipt for your purchases.
- Never sign a blank form or application. Make sure you understand what you are signing.
- For more information on common scams, please visit www.uscis.gov/uscis-tags/unassigned/avoid-scams.

Identity Theft
Identity theft is what happens when someone steals your personal information, such as your Social Security or bank account number. They can use it to pretend to be you, and take money from your bank account, get a credit card in your name, or take other benefits that belong to you. This can cause problems for many years, and is a very serious crime.

CHAPTER 22

Protect yourself from identity theft by taking the following steps:

- Make sure you know and trust the people or businesses you give your personal information to, especially on the phone or Internet.
- Keep your Social Security card and other confidential, personal documents at home in a safe place.
- Carry only the bank or credit cards, checks, and documents you need with you at the time. Leave the rest at home in a safe place.
- Shred any documents that have your credit card numbers, bank account, or Social Security number on them before throwing them in the trash. Be sure to inspect your mail for these numbers before you throw it away—bank statements and loan statements often have this information.

For tips on avoiding identity theft, please go to the Federal Trade Commission's website at www.consumer.ftc.gov/features/feature-0014-identity-theft.

CHAPTER 23

How to Get Emotional Support

Introduction

It is not easy to adjust to a new culture. Especially when you are not with your whole family, learning to live in the U.S. can be very difficult. Be patient with yourself and those people around you. Do you have trouble sleeping? Have you lost your appetite? Are you having trouble concentrating? Can you not stop thinking about painful memories? These are normal reactions to stressful events. But if these reactions get too strong or affect your ability to do anything else, they can make it more difficult to adjust to living in the U.S.

Mental and Emotional Health

Mental health includes many factors, including how we think, feel, and act. Mental health also impacts how we handle stress, relate to others, and make choices. Mental health is important to every person, from children to older generations.

As a newcomer, you may feel helpless and frustrated living in a country you do not understand. It is common for anyone living in a new place to have these feelings. It is common to feel frustrated because doing simple things like shopping or taking public transportation feels very difficult. You may feel tired during the day or unable to sleep at night. You may also just feel sad without knowing why. Many newcomers do not feel like eating and experience some memory loss.

You may also experience some physical symptoms as a result of these emotions. If you have a headache or stomachache that does not go away, it may be related to your emotional health. While many of these symptoms are common to newcomers, they can also be the result of trauma from past experiences. It is important to your overall health and well-being to seek support if you are having a difficult time coping with these feelings.

Importance of Mental Health in the U.S.

Americans believe that mental health is as important as physical health, and that good health care includes treatment by a doctor when it is needed. It is important to pay special attention to your mental health, especially if you experienced difficult events in the past. Adjusting to life in the U.S. can be very stressful.

Seeking emotional support is common in the U.S. and openly accepted. Many people find it helpful to talk to a counselor or support group. The first time you can listen or just talk a little. You can share more as you feel comfortable. In the U.S. we recognize that, depending on what is happening in our life, we all may need support at some time.

How to Get Support

If you ever feel that life is too hard and you cannot deal with everyday activities, you should seek help. There are many organizations that can help you find services, and will keep your information confidential.

HOW TO GET EMOTIONAL SUPPORT

Many people who have lived through similar situations find it helpful to talk about their memories. You may find it helpful to talk with others who have gone through experiences similar to yours or with people who have learned how to live in the U.S. You can find support groups or mental and emotional service providers such as counselors by calling the agencies listed in Chapter 25, "Directory of Resettlement Agencies (RAs)," and Chapter 26, "Directory of Torture Treatment Providers."

State Health Coordinator (For Refugees)

Each state has a Refugee Health Coordinator who should know what health programs and services are available in your local area. You can find your state's Refugee Health Coordinator by calling the Office of Refugee Resettlement at 1-202-401-9246 or by going online to http://www.acf.hhs.gov/programs/orr/resource/orr-funded-programs-key-contacts.

Refugee Medical Assistance (RMA)

Mental health services may be available to you through Refugee Medical Assistance (RMA). See Chapter 19, "How to Access Healthcare," to see if you are eligible for RMA. If you want to speak with a trained specialist or counselor, RMA usually covers the cost of counseling or other mental health services for the first eight months after you are admitted as a refugee or are granted an eligible status.

The Substance Abuse and Mental Health Service Administration (SAMHSA)

SAMHSA is a public health agency of the U.S. government. SAMHSA helps to connect people with mental and emotional care. SAMHSA also helps people who have mental illness or who are recovering from using drugs or too much alcohol and tobacco. The SAMHSA website has a mental health facility locator that has the contact information for counseling services and other mental health services. You can find the locator online at http://store.samhsa.gov/mhlocator or you can call 1-877-726-4727 (1-877-SAMHSA7).

Calling "211"

You can call 211 on your phone in many states to get help finding the services you need. This service can connect you to many resources, including mental health services.

Emergency Suicide Prevention

Sometimes, people become so depressed they can feel like there is no way out, and they feel they want to end their life. If you, or someone you know, ever feels like this, **seek help immediately.** The following National Suicide Prevention Hotline numbers are operated by the Substance Abuse and Mental Health Services Administration of the Department of Health and Human Services:

1-800-SUICIDE (1-800-784-2433)
1-888-SUICIDE (1-888-784-2433)
1-877-SUICIDA (1-877-784-2432) (Spanish)

Helpful Terms to Know

- ***Mental health:*** How you feel, think, and behave as you deal with life. It also refers to how you handle stress.
- ***Stress:*** Emotional or mental strain or tension resulting from demanding, scary, or heavy circumstances. It may be an immediate reaction to a situation, such as dropping a bag of groceries or getting lost. Or it can last a long time if you're dealing with serious problems such as the death of a loved one, loss of a job, or being a migrant and having to move

to different places and not knowing your future. Stress becomes dangerous when it interferes with your ability to live a normal life over an extended period. You may feel tired, unable to concentrate, or irritable. Stress can also damage your physical health.

- ***Trauma:*** An emotional response to a terrible event such as an accident, physical attack, incident of torture, death of a loved one, or natural disaster. Immediately after the event, many people are in shock or cannot accept that the event happened. You might have reactions that last weeks, months, or even years. These reactions might include unpredictable emotions, difficulty concentrating and relating to other people, or physical symptoms such as headaches or stomachaches. It is normal to have these reactions. It is helpful to see a psychologist or therapist, who can help you find ways to deal with this trauma so it does not prevent you from living a normal life.

CHAPTER 24

Religious, Cultural, and Community Groups

As you begin to establish your new life in the U.S., you may find you want to connect with people in your community or from your cultural or ethnic group. You may want to find people who practice the same religion as you. You may want to find places where you can learn English. Finding groups in your community may make it easier to adjust to life in the U.S. These groups can help if you feel alone or confused or just want to find friends. There are many ways to find community and cultural groups.

There are organizations in many communities that provide free or low-cost assistance to immigrants. These organizations can help you learn about your community and the services available to you.

Private Assistance Organizations

These organizations provide services that help newcomers. Many communities offer services such as counseling, immigration assistance, English classes, help finding a job, and translation services. Local religious organizations or community centers are great places to connect with other people. Two common types of private assistance organizations are community-based organizations and faith-based organizations.

Community-Based Organizations (CBOs)

These organizations operate in a community and provide recreational, social, and educational services to community members. One type of CBO that you may find in your community is an ethnic community-based organization (ECBO). There are a number of national organizations made up of refugees and other migrants who help members of their ethnic community to integrate into life in the U.S. They may be able to help you learn what is available in your local community and help you get involved. You can learn more about ECBOs in your area by calling the Office of Refugee Resettlement at 202-401-9246 or by going online to www.acf.hhs.gov/programs/orr/resource/ethnic-community-self-help-grants.

Faith-Based Organizations

Houses of worship and religious groups are often involved in refugee resettlement and immigrant services. Churches, mosques, synagogues, and other religious groups may also offer assistance and support. Some religious organizations such as churches can help people find housing, clothing, or food. You do not have to participate in the group's religious activities to receive services.

Community Groups and Events

Getting involved in your community will help you feel more at home in the U.S. Your community is also a good source of information. You can get involved in your community by joining your neighborhood association. This is a group of people in the neighborhood who meet to improve the neighborhood. Learning English will also help you feel more comfortable. You can find more ideas about getting involved on the Department of Housing and Urban Development's website at www.hud.gov.

City Resources

Some cities have a department that focuses on cultural groups and events in the community. It may be called the "Immigrant Affairs Office" or "Office of Multicultural Affairs." Other cities may have a person called the "Community Liaison" or the "Diversity Liaison." You can go to your city's website or call them to find if they have a liaison that can connect you with cultural groups in your area.

You can also check out the list of programs on the National Partnership for New Americans website. These programs provide support to immigrants, refugees, and lawful permanent residents. To see the list, visit www.partnershipfornewamericans.org/new-americans-programs/.

Local Events

Community newspapers often list a calendar of local events where you can meet people who share a similar interest. Community Colleges and local libraries are great places to look for different kinds of groups that may be in your area.

Cultural Orientation Resource Center

The Cultural Orientation Resource (COR) Center offers workshops, trainings, and other material that may help you adjust to life in the U.S. COR Center has published a guidebook to help refugees adjust to life in the U.S. called "Welcome to the U.S.: Guidebook for Refugees." The guidebook can be found online in 12 different languages at www.culturalorientation.net.

CHAPTER 25

Directory of Resettlement Agencies (RAs)

The following organizations are resettlement agencies (RAs). They used to be called voluntary resettlement agencies (VOLAGs) so you may hear them called either VOLAGs or RAs. These national agencies help connect asylees with many of the services discussed in this guide. Most of the agencies listed below will refer you to a local organization to contact.

Church World Service (CWS), Immigration and Refugee Program
1-800-297-1516
www.churchworldservice.org

Episcopal Migration Ministries (EMM)
1-800-334-7626
www.ecusa.anglican.org/emm

Ethiopian Community Development Council (ECDC)
703-685-0510
www.ecdcinternational.org

CHAPTER 25

Hebrew Immigrant Aid Society (HIAS)
1-800-442-7714
www.hias.org

International Rescue Committee (IRC)
212-551-3000
www.theirc.org

Kurdish Human Rights Watch, Inc. (KHRW)
703-385-3806
www.khrw.org

Lutheran Immigration and Refugee Service (LIRS)
410-230-2700
www.lirs.org

U.S. Committee for Refugees and Immigrants (USCRI)
703-310-1130
www.refugees.org

United States Conference of Catholic Bishops (USCCB)
Migration and Refugee Services
202-541-3352
www.usccb.org/about/migration-and-refugee-services/

World Relief Corporation (WRRS)
1-800-535-5433
www.wr.org

CHAPTER 26

Directory of Torture Treatment Providers

The following organizations care for survivors of torture. They help with survivors' special needs, including emotional support and community services. They are listed in alphabetical order by state. Find the organization closest to you and call to ask about the services they offer.

National Organizations

The following national organizations have an extensive online database with additional resources for torture survivors. If you cannot find a service provider who can help you listed under your state below, call one of these national organizations and ask them to find someone who can help you, or visit them online.

Detained Torture Survivors' Legal Support Network
Lutheran Immigration and Refugee Service
700 Light Street, Baltimore, MD 212130
410-230-2700
www.lirs.org

CHAPTER 26

Heal Torture
www.healtorture.org

National Consortium of Torture Treatment Programs
www.ncttp.org

Torture Abolition and Survivors Support Coalition International (TASSC)
202-529-2991
www.tassc.org

Substance Abuse and Mental Health Services Administration
24-hour mental health referral service: 1-800-662-HELP (4357), TTY: 1-800-487-4889
www.samhsa.gov/treatment/index.aspx

Alabama
There are currently no torture survivor support centers located in Alabama. Speak with your caseworker or legal service provider to identify emotional support and community services in your area. The groups below may be able to help or provide referrals:

Catholic Social Services
400 Government Street, Mobile, AL 36602
251-434-1550
www.catholicsocialservicesmobile.com/cssmob/

MHA (Mental Health America) in Montgomery
1116 S. Hull St.
Montgomery, AL 36104
334-262-5500
www.mhamontgomery.com

DIRECTORY OF TORTURE TREATMENT PROVIDERS

Alaska

There are currently no torture survivor support centers located in Alaska. Speak with your case worker or legal service provider to identify emotional support and community services in your area. The group below may be able to help or provide referrals:

National Alliance on Mental Illness (NAMI) Anchorage
144 W. 15th Street, Anchorage, AK 99501
907-272-0227
www.nami.org/sites/alaska

Arizona

International Rescue Committee Tucson Center for Well-Being
3100 N Campbell Suite #101, Tucson, AZ 85719
520-319-2128
www.rescue.org/us-program/us-tucson-az

Arkansas

There are currently no torture survivor support centers located in Arkansas. Speak with your case worker or legal service provider to identify emotional support and community services in your area. The groups below may be able to help or provide referrals:

National Alliance on Mental Illness (NAMI) Arkansas
1012 Autumn Road, Suite 1, Little Rock, AR 72211
501-661-1548
www.namiarkansas.org/home

MHA (Mental Health America) of Northwest Arkansas
P.O. Box 4714, Fayetteville, AR 72702
479-575-2817
srausch@uark.edu

California

The Center for Justice and Accountability
870 Market Street, Suite 680, San Francisco, CA 94102
415-544-0444
www.cja.org

Center for Survivors of Torture (AACI)
2400 Moorpark Ave, Suite #300, San Jose, CA 95128
408-975-2730
cst.aaci.org

Chaldean-Middle Eastern Social Services
436 S. Magnolia Ave, Suite #201 El Cajon, CA 92020
619-631-7400
www.c-mss.org/

Legal Aid Foundation of Los Angeles
Torture Survivors Project
1102 Crenshaw Blvd, Los Angeles, CA 90019
1-800-399-4529
www.lafla.org/service.php?sect=immigrate&sub=torture&msect=main

Program for Torture Victims
3655 S. Grand Ave, Suite #290, Los Angeles, CA, 90007
213-747-4944
www.ptvla.org

DIRECTORY OF TORTURE TREATMENT PROVIDERS

Survivors International: Trauma Recovery Center
727 Mariposa Street, Suite 100, San Francisco, CA 94110
415-437-3000
http://traumarecoverycenter.org/services/survivors-international/

Survivors of Torture International
P.O. Box 151240, San Diego, CA 92175-1240
619-278-2400
www.notorture.org

Colorado

Catholic Charities – Archdiocese of Denver
4045 Pecos Street, Denver, Colorado 80211
303-742-0828
http://www.ccdenver.org/

Jewish Family Service of Colorado
3201 South Tamarac Drive, Denver, CO 80231
303-597-5000
http://jewishfamilyservice.org/

Lutheran Family Services Rocky Mountains
1600 Downing Street, Suite 600, Denver, CO 80218
303-980-5400, or 1-877-372-1264
www.lfsrm.org/

Connecticut

Khmer Health Advocates
1125 New Britain Ave, Suite 202, West Hartford, CT 06110
860-561-3345

Mental Health Association of Connecticut
61 South Main Street, Suite #100, West Hartford, CT 06107
860-529-1970 ext. 117
www.mhact.org

International Institute of Connecticut
670 Clinton Avenue, Bridgeport, CT 06605
203-336-0141
http://iiconn.org

Delaware
There are currently no torture survivor support centers located in Delaware. Speak with your case worker or legal service provider to identify emotional support and community services in your area. The groups below may be able to help or provide referrals:

Catholic Charities – Diocese of Wilmington
2601 W Fourth Street, Wilmington, Delaware 19905
302-655-9624
http://www.cdow.org/

Mental Health Association in Delaware
100 West 10th Street, Suite 600, Wilmington, DE 19801
302-654-6833
www.mhainde.org

District of Columbia (Washington D.C.)

Advocates for Survivors of Torture and Trauma
1624 U Street NW, Washington, DC 20009
202-290-1672
www.astt.org

DIRECTORY OF TORTURE TREATMENT PROVIDERS

Center for Victims of Torture
1776 K Street Northwest, Washington, DC 20006
202-822-0188
http://cvt.org

TASSC International
4121 Harewood Road Northeast, Washington, DC 20017
202-529-2991
http://tassc.org

Florida

Florida Center for Survivors of Torture (A program of Jewish Family Services)
14041 Icot Boulevard, Clearwater, Florida 33760
727-479-1800
http://gulfcoastjewishfamilyandcommunityservices.org/refugee/

Georgia

Center for Torture and Trauma Survivors, Inc.
3700 Market Street, Building B, Clarkston, GA
770-222-6622 ext. 300

Hawaii

There are currently no torture survivor support centers located in Hawaii. Speak with your case worker or legal service provider to identify emotional support and community services in your area. The groups below may be able to help or provide referrals:

Catholic Charities Hawaii
1822 Keeaumoku Street, Honolulu, HI 96822
808-524-4673
www.catholiccharitieshawaii.org

MHA (Mental Health America) of Hawaii
1124 Fort Street Mall, Room 205, Honolulu, HI 96813
808-521-1846
www.mentalhealth-hi.org

Idaho

There are currently no torture survivor support centers located in Idaho. Speak with your case worker or legal service provider to identify emotional support and community services in your area. The groups below may be able to help or provide referrals:

Catholic Charities of Idaho
847 Park Centre Way, Suite 7, Nampa, ID 83651
208-466-9926
www.ccidaho.org

Mountain States Group – Agency for New Americans
1614 W. Jefferson Street, Boise, ID 83702
208-338-0033
www.mtnstatesgroup.org/

Illinois

The Interfaith Committee for Detained Immigrants
10024 S. Central Park Ave, Chicago, IL 60655
773-779-6011 ext. 3846
www.icdichicago.org/

DIRECTORY OF TORTURE TREATMENT PROVIDERS

The Marjorie Kovler Center for the Treatment of Survivors of Torture
1331 West Albion Ave, Chicago, IL
773-381-4070
www.heartlandalliance.org/kovler/

Indiana

There are currently no torture survivor support centers located in Indiana. Speak with your case worker or legal service provider to identify emotional support and community services in your area. The groups below may be able to help or provide referrals:

St. Vincent Indianapolis Stress Center
8401 Harcourt Road, Indianapolis IN 46260
317-338-4800
www.stvincent.org/St-Vincent-Indianapolis/Healthcare-Services/Mental-And-Behavioral-Health.aspx

MHA (Mental Health America) of Indiana
1431 North Delaware St., Indianapolis, IN 46202
800-555-6424
https://mhai.net/

Iowa

There are currently no torture survivor support centers located in Iowa. Speak with your case worker or legal service provider to identify emotional support and community services in your area. The groups below may be able to help or provide referrals:

Lutheran Services in Iowa
1323 Northwestern Ave, Ames, IA 50010
515-232-7262
http://lsiowa.org

Mental Health Association of Siouxland
2523 Myrtle St., Sioux City, IA 51103
712-255-1691
www.hopetalks.com

Kansas

There are currently no torture survivor support centers located in Kansas. Speak with your case worker or legal service provider to identify emotional support and community services in your area. The groups below may be able to help or provide referrals:

Catholic Charities of Northern Kansas
425 W. Iron Ave, P.O. Box 1366, Salina, KS 67402-1366
785-825-0208
www.ccnks.org/index.php

MHA (Mental Health America) of the Heartland
739 Minnesota Ave., Kansas City, KS 66101-2703
913-281-2221
www.mhah.org/index.html

Kentucky

There are currently no torture survivor support centers located in Kentucky. Speak with your case worker or legal service provider to identify emotional support and community services in your area. The groups below may be able to help or provide referrals:

Catholic Charities of Louisville, Inc.
St. Charles, 100 Melonie Street, Suite F, Boutte, KY
985-785-2113
www.cclou.org/

DIRECTORY OF TORTURE TREATMENT PROVIDERS

Survivors of Torture Recovery Center (STRC)
4803 Southside Drive, Louisville, KY 40214
http://louisville.edu/kent/RESEARCH/recent-awards/survivors-of-torture-recovery-center-strc

Louisiana

There are currently no torture survivor support centers located in Louisiana. Speak with your case worker or legal service provider to identify emotional support and community services in your area. The groups below may be able to help or provide referrals:

Catholic Charities of New Orleans – Immigrant Survivors Service
1000 Howard Ave, 2nd Floor, New Orleans, LA 70113
504-310-8765
www.ccano.org

MHA (Mental Health America) of Louisiana
5700 Florida Blvd, Suite 1212, Baton Rouge, LA 70806
225-978-2176
www.mentalhealthamerica.net/mhala

Maine

Refugee Services, City of Portland, Maine
190 Lancaster Street, Portland, Maine 04101
207-775-7915
www.portlandmaine.gov/855/Refugee-Services

Maryland

Advocates for Survivors of Torture and Trauma
431 E. Belvedere Ave, Baltimore, MD 21212

410-464-9006
www.astt.org

Massachusetts

Boston Center for Refugee Health and Human Rights
Boston Medical Center
771 Albany Street, Dowling 7, Boston, MA 02118
617-414-4794
www.bcrhhr.org

Harvard Program in Refugee Trauma
22 Putnam Avenue, Cambridge, MA 02139
617-876-7879
www.hprt-cambridge.org

International Survivors Center, c/o International Institute of New England
1 Milk Street, 4th Floor, Boston, MA 02109
617-695-9990
www.iine.us

Lowell Community Health Center
Multicultural Connections for Health
161 Jackson Street, Lowell, MA 01852
978-322-8536
www.lchealth.org/patients/connect-services/community-health-programs

Ascentria Care Alliance
51 Union St, Suite 222, Worcester, MA 01608
508-754-1121
http://www.ascentria.org

Refugee and Asylum and Assistance Project
Community Legal Services and Counseling Center
1 West Street, Cambridge, MA, 02139
617-661-1010
www.clsacc.org

Refugee Immigration Ministry
142 Pleasant Street, Suite 203, Malden, MA 02148
781-322-1011
www.r-i-m.net/

Michigan

ACCESS Psychosocial Rehabilitation Center
2651 Saulino Court, Dearborn, MI 48120
313-842-7010
www.accesscommunity.org

The Refugee Center for Healing Torture and Trauma
901 Eastern Ave. NE, PO Box 294, Grand Rapids, MI 49501-0294
616-224-7550
www.bethany.org/refugeehealingcenter

Trauma Recovery Center of Southeast Michigan
34628 Dequindre, Suite 2, Sterling Heights, Michigan 48310
586-939-5016
http://psychiatry.med.wayne.edu/trauma-center.php

CHAPTER 26

Minnesota

The Center for Victims of Torture
649 Dayton Ave, St. Paul, MN 55114
612-436-4840
www.cvt.org

Guadalupe Alternative Programs
381 East Robie Street, St. Paul, MN 55107
651-222-0757
www.gapschool.org/index.html

Minnesota Advocates for Human Rights
330 Second Avenue South, Suite 800, Minneapolis, MN 55401
612-341-3302
www.mnadvocates.org

Psychological Services - University of St. Thomas
Interpersonal Center, 2115 Summit Avenue, St. Paul, Minnesota 55105
651-962-4820
www.stthomas.edu/counseling

Sarah's OASIS
Highland Park, St. Paul, MN
651-696-8699
http://sarahsoasis.org/

St. Stephen's Human Services
2309 Nicollet Avenue South, Minneapolis, MN 55404
612-874-0311
http://ststephensmpls.org/

DIRECTORY OF TORTURE TREATMENT PROVIDERS

Mississippi

There are currently no torture survivor support centers located in Mississippi. Speak with your case worker or legal service provider to identify emotional support and community services in your area. The groups below may be able to help or provide referrals:

Catholic Charities of Jackson – Immigration Clinic
200 N. Congress Street, Suite 100, Jackson, MS 39201
601-948-2635
www.catholiccharitiesjackson.org

Mental Health Association of South Mississippi
4803 Harrison Circle, Gulfport, MS 39507
228-864-6274
www.msmentalhealth.org/

Missouri

Center for Survivors of Torture and War Trauma
1077 S. Newstead Ave, St. Louis, MO 63110
314-533-4114
http://stlcenterforsurvivors.org

St. Louis Mental Health Board / St. Louis Survivors Collaborative
4144 Lindell Blvd, Suite 300, Saint Louis, MO 63108
314-535-6964
www.stlmhb.com

The Center for Trauma Recovery (CTR)
University of Missouri-St. Louis, One University Boulevard, St. Louis, MO 63121-4499
314-516-6737
www.umsl.edu/divisions/artscience/psychology/ctr/

CHAPTER 26

Montana

There are currently no torture survivor support centers located in Montana. Speak with your case worker or legal service provider to identify emotional support and community services in your area. The groups below may be able to help or provide referrals:

Glacier Community Health Center
519 East Main Street, Cut Bank, MT 59427
406-873-5670
www.glacierchc.org/index.php

MHA (Mental Health America) of Montana
P.O. Box 88, Bozeman, MT 59771-0088
406-587-7774
www.montanamentalhealth.org/

Nebraska

There are currently no torture survivor support centers located in Nebraska. Speak with your case worker or legal service provider to identify emotional support and community services in your area. The groups below may be able to help or provide referrals:

Lutheran Family Services – Lutheran Immigration Services
1811 W. 2nd St, Suite 365, Grand Island, NE 68803
308-382-4255
www.lfsneb.org/community/immigration.asp

Mental Health Association of Nebraska
1645 N Street, Suite A, Lincoln, NE 68508
888-902-2822
www.mha-ne.org/

DIRECTORY OF TORTURE TREATMENT PROVIDERS

Nevada

There are currently no torture survivor support centers located in Nevada. Speak with your case worker or legal service provider to identify emotional support and community services in your area. The groups below may be able to help or provide referrals:

Catholic Charities of Northern Nevada, St. Vincent's Center
500 E. 4th St, Reno, NV 89512
775-322-7073
http://ccnnimmigration.wordpress.com

Northern Nevada HOPES Clinic
580 W 5th Street, 12C, Reno, NV 89503
775-786-4673
www.nnhopes.org/

New Hampshire

There are currently no torture survivor support centers located in New Hampshire. Speak with your case worker or legal service provider to identify emotional support and community services in your area. The groups below may be able to help or provide referrals:

New Hampshire Catholic Charities – Immigration and Refugee Services
325 Franklin St, Manchester, NH 03101
603-624-4717
www.nh-cc.org

National Alliance on Mental Illness (NAMI) of New Hampshire
85 North State St., Concord, NH 03301
603-225-5359
www.naminh.org

Riverbend Community Mental Health
278 Pleasant Street, Concord, NH 03301
603-228-1600
http://riverbendcmhc.org

New Jersey

American Friends Service Committee
89 Market Street, 6th Floor, Newark, NJ 07102
973-643-1924
http://afsc.org/office/newark-nj

Catholic Charities of the Archdiocese of Newark
590 North 7th Street, Newark, NJ 07107
973-596-4100
www.ccannj.com/index.php

First Friends
53 So. Hackensack Ave, Kearny, NJ 07032908-965-0455
http://firstfriendsnjny.org/

New Mexico
There are currently no torture survivor support centers located in New Mexico. Speak with your case worker or legal service provider to identify emotional support and community services in your area. The groups below may be able to help or provide referrals:

Catholic Charities of New Mexico
2010 Bridge Blvd SW, Albuquerque, NM 87105
505-247-0442
www.ccasfnm.org/

The Life Link
2325 Cerrillos Road, Santa Fe, NM 87505
505-438-0010
http://thelifelink.org/

Lutheran Family Services Rocky Mountains
3612 Campus Blvd. NE, Albuquerque, NM 87106
505-933-7032
www.lfsrm.org

New York

Bellevue/NYU Program for Survivors of Torture
462 1st Avenue, New York, NY 10010
212-683-7446
www.survivorsoftorture.org

HealthRight International
65 Broadway, 19th Floor, New York, NY 10006
212-226-9890
www.healthright.org

Hebrew Immigrant Service Committee (HIAS)
333 Seventh Avenue, 16th Floor, New York, NY 10001
212-967-4100
www.hias.org/en

Libertas Center for Human Rights
Elmhurst Hospital, Annex G, 5th floor 79-01 Broadway Ave, Elmhurst, NY
718-334-6209
www.libertascenter.net

CHAPTER 26

Journey's End Refugee Services
2495 Main Street, #317, Buffalo, NY 14214
716-882-4963
www.jersbuffalo.org/

My Sisters' Place
1 Water Street, White Plains, NY 10601
914-358-0333
http://mspny.org/

New York Immigration Hotline
Can provide referrals throughout NY State.
1-800-566-7636 or 212-419-3737

REFUGE
International Trauma Studies Program
245 5th Avenue, Suite 2205, New York, NY 10016
212-889-8117
www.itspnyc.org

Safe Horizon
Brooklyn, New York, NY
Counseling Center: 347-328-8110
Immigration Law Project: 718-943-8632
www.safehorizon.org

Seafarers International House
123 East 15th Street, New York, NY 10003
212-677-4800
www.sihnyc.org/index.php

USCRI Albany
991 Broadway #223, Albany, NY 12204
518-459-1790
www.refugees.org/about-us/where-we-work/albany/

North Carolina

There are currently no torture survivor support centers located in North Carolina. Speak with your caseworker or legal service provider to identify emotional support and community services in your area. The groups below may be able to help or provide referrals:

Catholic Charities of the Diocese of Raleigh
7200 Stonehenge Drive, Raleigh, NC 27613
919-821-9750
www.catholiccharitiesraleigh.org/

Lutheran Family Services in the Carolinas
Charlotte Counseling Center
1001 Queens Road, Charlotte, NC 28207
980-613-3400
www.lfscarolinas.org/

North Dakota

There are currently no torture survivor support centers located in North Dakota. Speak with your case worker or legal service provider to identify emotional support and community services in your area. The groups below may be able to help or provide referrals:

Catholic Charities North Dakota
5201 Bishops Blvd, Suite B, Fargo, ND 58104
701-235-4457
919 7th St. S, Suite 607, Bismarck, ND 58504

701-255-1793
http://catholiccharitiesnd.org/

MHA (Mental Health America) of North Dakota
PO Box 4106, Bismarck, ND 58502
1-800-472-2911
www.mhand.org/

Ohio

There are currently no torture survivor support centers located in Ohio. Speak with your case worker or legal service provider to identify emotional support and community services in your area. The groups below may be able to help or provide referrals:

Catholic Charities of Southwestern Ohio
100 E. 8th Street, Cincinnati, OH 45202
513-241-7745
http://ccswoh.org/

National Alliance on Mental Illness (NAMI) Ohio
1225 Dublin Road, Suite 125, Columbus, OH 43215
614-224-2700
www.namiohio.org/

Oklahoma

Catholic Charities of Oklahoma City – Immigration Assistance Program
1501 N. Classen Blvd, Oklahoma City, OK 73106
405-523-3001
www.catholiccharitiesok.org

The Center for Survivors of Torture
5124 Burnet Road, Austin, TX 78756
512-358-4612
www.cstnet.org

Oregon

Torture Treatment Center of Oregon
Portland, Oregon
503-494-4222
www.ohsu.edu

Pennsylvania

Nationalities Service Center
1216 Arch Street, Philadelphia, PA 19107
215-893–8400
www.nationalitiesservice.org/

Rhode Island

There are currently no torture survivor support centers located in Rhode Island. Speak with your case worker or legal service provider to identify emotional support and community services in your area. The groups below may be able to help or provide referrals:

Catholic Charities of Providence
1 Cathedral Square, Providence, RI 02903
401-421-7833 ext. 129
www.diocesepvd.org/charitableministries/immigration-refugee-services/

Rhode Island Free Clinic
655 Broad Street, Providence, RI 02907
401-274-6347
http://rifreeclinic.org/

South Carolina

There are currently no torture survivor support centers located in South Carolina. Speak with your case worker or legal service provider to identify emotional support and community services in your area. The groups below may be able to help or provide referrals:

HopeHealth, Inc.
600 E. Palmetto Street, PO Box 653, Florence, SC 29506
843-667-9414
http://hope-health.org/home.aspx

Lutheran Family Services in the Carolinas
Cauble Center
1118 Union Street, Columbia, SC 29201
803-750-9917
www.lfscarolinas.org/

South Dakota

There are currently no torture survivor support centers located in South Dakota. Speak with your case worker or legal service provider to identify emotional support and community services in your area. The groups below may be able to help or provide referrals:

Avera Behavioral Health Center
2412 South Cliff Ave, Sioux Falls, SD 57108
605-322-4079
www.avera.org/

Catholic Social Services
529 Kansas City Street, Suite #100, Rapid City, SD 57701
605-348-6086
www.catholicsocialservicesrapidcity.com

Tennessee

There are currently no torture survivor support centers located in Tennessee. Speak with your case worker or legal service provider to identify emotional support and community services in your area. The groups below may be able to help or provide referrals:

Catholic Charities of Tennessee, Inc.
30 White Bridge Road, Nashville, TN 37205
615-352-3087
www.cctenn.org/

Hope Family Health
12124 Hwy 52W, Westmoreland, TN 37186
615-644-2000
http://hopefamilyhealth.org

Texas

The Center for Survivors of Torture
4102 Swiss Avenue, Dallas, TX 75204
214-827-2314
5124 Burnet Road, Austin, TX 78756
512-358-4612
www.cstnet.org

CHAPTER 26

Utah

Refugee and Immigrant Center – Asian Association of Utah
Asian Association of Utah
155 South 300 West, Salt Lake City, UT 84101
801-467-6060
www.aau-slc.org

Utah Health and Human Rights Project
225 South 200 East, Suite 250, Salt Lake City, UT 84111
801-363-4596
www.uhhr.org/

Vermont

New England Survivors of Torture and Trauma
The Behavior Therapy and Psychotherapy Center
University of Vermont, Room 135 John Dewey Hall, 2 Colchester Ave, Burlington, VT 05405
802-656-2661
http://newenglandsurvivorsoftorture.org

Virginia

Program for Survivors of Torture and Severe Trauma (PSTT)
(A program of Northern Virginia Family Service)
6400 Arlington Blvd. Suite 110, Falls Church, VA 22042
571-748-2823
www.nvfs.org/pstt

Boat People SOS
6066 Leesburg Pike, Suite 100, Falls Church, VA 22041
703-538-2190
www.bpsos.org

Washington (Washington State)

Northwest Detention Center Roundtable
621 Tacoma Ave South, Suite 501, Tacoma, WA 98402
nwdcr.info@gmail.com
http://nwdcroundtable.org
Meets at St. Leo's Church in Tacoma
710 S 13th St, Tacoma, WA 98405
www.stleoparish.org

Lutheran Community Services Northwest: Pathways to Wellness
4040 S. 188th St SeaTac, WA 98188
206-838-2680
www.lcsnw.org/pathways/

Washington, D.C. (listed under "District of Columbia" above)

West Virginia
There are currently no torture survivor support centers located in West Virginia. Speak with your case worker or legal service provider to identify emotional support and community services in your area. The following groups may be able to help or offer referrals:

Catholic Charities West Virginia
2000 Main Street, Wheeling, WV 26003
304-905-9860
www.catholiccharitieswv.org/index.php

Shenandoah Valley Medical System, Inc.
Behavioral Health Services
130 Augustine Ave, Charles Town, WV 25414
304-728-3716
www.svms.net/index.php

Wisconsin

International Institute of Wisconsin
1110 N. Old World 3rd St, Suite 420, Milwaukee, WI 53203
414-225-6220
www.iiwisconsin.org

National Alliance on Mental Illness (NAMI) Dane County
United Way Building, 2059 Atwood Ave, Fourth Floor, Madison, WI 53704
608-249-7188
www.namidanecounty.org/

Wyoming

There are currently no torture survivor support centers located in West Virginia. Speak with your caseworker or legal service provider to identify emotional support and community services in your area. The following groups may be able to help or offer referrals:

DIRECTORY OF TORTURE TREATMENT PROVIDERS

Northern Wyoming Mental Health
1221 West 5th St., Sheridan, WY 82801
307-674-4405
http://wyomentalhealth.org/

Wyoming Coalition Against Domestic Violence and Sexual Assault
PO Box 236 710 Garfield Street, Suite 218, Laramie, WY 82073
307-755-5481
www.wyomingdvsa.org/

CHAPTER 27

Directory of Immigration Legal Services Providers

The following organizations are free or low-cost immigration legal service providers. They offer a variety of legal services, including assistance completing immigration related forms, filings with USCIS, representation at asylum interviews, and/or representation before immigration court. Find the organization closest to you and call to ask about the services they offer and fees charged. **There are many more organizations than we have listed here. Please visit the following sites to find organizations in your area:**

- Immigration Law Help: www.immigrationlawhelp.org/ (search by state)
- EOIR Free Legal Services Provider List: www.justice.gov/eoir/probono/states.htm (search by state)
- AILA (American Immigration Lawyers Association) Immigration Lawyer Referral Service: www.ailalawyer.com, (202-216-2400)
- National Lawyers Guild, National Immigration Project: www.nationalimmigrationproject.org, (617-227-9727)

CHAPTER 27

Alabama

Catholic Social Services of Mobile
23010 Hwy 59 N, Robertsdale, AL 36567
251-947-3878
www.cssbaldwin.org

Alaska

Alaska Immigration Justice Project
431 W. 7th Ave, Suite 208, Anchorage, AK 99501
907-279-2457
www.akijp.org/

Arizona

Arizona Immigrant and Refugee Services
10240 N. 31st Ave, Suite 112, Phoenix, AZ 85051
602-944-1821
http://airsaz.org/

Florence Immigrant and Refugee Rights Project
2601 N. Pinal Pkwy, Florence, AZ 85132
520-868-0191
202 E. McDowell Rd, Suite 165, Phoenix, AZ 85004
602-307-1008
www.firrp.org/

Friendly House, Inc.
723 S. 1st Ave, Phoenix, AZ 85004
602-416-7200
www.friendlyhouse.org

DIRECTORY OF IMMIGRATION LEGAL SERVICES PROVIDERS

Arkansas

Catholic Charities Immigration Services
2500 N. Tyler St, P.O. BOX 7565, Little Rock, AR 72217
501-664-0340
www.dolr.org/offices/catholiccharities/immigration.php

Arkansas Justice for Our Neighbors
Dover United Methodist Church
81 W. Water Street, Dover, AR 72837
479-430-2223
First United Methodist Church
317 S. Main Street, Monticello, AR 71655
870-367-0407
www.ajfon.org

California

ABA Immigration Justice Project of San Diego
401 B St, Suite 1700, San Diego, CA 92101
619-699-2933
www.americanbar.org/ijp

Access California Services
2180 W. Crescent Ave, Suite C, Anaheim, CA 92801
714-917-0440
www.accesscal.org

California Rural Legal Assistance
Fill out the contact form (www.crla.org/contact-us) or call 805-922-4563 to ask for your local office.
www.crla.org

Casa Cornelia Law Center
2760 5th Ave., Suite 200, San Diego, CA 92103
619-231-7788
www.casacornelia.org

Catholic Charities CYO – Refugee & Immigrant Services
180 Howard St., Suite 100, San Francisco, CA 94105
415-972-1313
http://community.cccyo.org/page.aspx?pid=269

Human Rights Project
201 S. Santa Fe Ave., Suite 101, Los Angeles, CA 90012
213-680-7801
www.hrproject.org

Immigration Center for Women and Children
634 S. Spring St., Suite 727, Los Angeles, CA 90014
213-614-1165
http://icwclaw.org

Colorado

Catholic Charities of Denver – Immigration Services
4045 Pecos Street, Denver, CO 80211
303-742-4971
www.ccdenver.org/services/immigration-services

DIRECTORY OF IMMIGRATION LEGAL SERVICES PROVIDERS

Colorado Legal Services
617 S. Nevada Ave, Colorado Springs, CO 80903
719-471-0380
www.coloradolegalservices.org

Immigrant Legal Center of Boulder County
948 North Street, Suite 8, Boulder, CO 80304
303-444-1522
www.boulderayuda.org

Rocky Mountain Immigrant Advocacy Network (RMIAN)
3489 W. 72nd Ave, Suite 211, Westminster, CO 80030
303-433-2812
www.rmian.org

Connecticut

Apostle Immigrant Services
81 Saltonstall Ave, New Haven, CT 06513
203-752-9068
www.apostleimmigrantservices.org

Catholic Charities of Fairfield County
238 Jewett Ave, Bridgeport, CT 06606
860-443-5328
http://www.ccfairfield.org/

The International Institute of Connecticut, Inc.
175 Main Street, Hartford, CT 06106
860-692-3085
http://iiconn.org

CHAPTER 27

Delaware

Catholic Charities Inc., Diocese of Wilmington
2601 W. 4th Street, Wilmington, DE 19805
302-655-9624
www.cdow.org/immigration.html

La Esperanza Community Center, Inc.
216 North Race Street, Georgetown, DE 19947
302-854-9262
www.laesperanza.org/

District of Columbia (Washington D.C.)

Capital Area Immigrants' Rights (CAIR) Coalition
1612 K Street NW, Suite 204, Washington, DC 20006
202-331-3320
www.caircoalition.org/

Catholic Charities Archdiocese of Washington
924 G St., NW, Washington, DC 20001
202-772-4300
www.catholiccharitiesdc.org/

Catholic Immigration Network (CLINIC)
8757 Georgia Ave, Suite 850, Silver Spring, MD 20910
301-565-4800
https://cliniclegal.org/

Central American Resource Center (CARECEN)
1460 Columbia Rd NW, Washington, DC 20009
202-328-9799
www.carecendc.org/

DIRECTORY OF IMMIGRATION LEGAL SERVICES PROVIDERS

KIND (Kids In Need of Defense)
1300 L St. NW, Suite 1100, Washington, DC 20005
202-824-8680
www.supportkind.org

Florida

CASA
10200 State Rd. 84, Suite 105, Davie, FL 33324
954-382-6000
10300 Sunset Drive, Suite 387, Miami, FL 33173
305-463-7468
www.casa-us.org

Catholic Charities of Central Florida – Immigration & Refugee Services
1771 N. Semoran Blvd, Suite C, Orlando, FL 32807
407-658-0110
www.cirsorl.org

Catholic Charities of Northwest Florida – Immigration & Refugee Services
1 N. C Street, Pensacola, FL 32502
850-436-6420
http://ccnwfl.org/

CHAPTER 27

Georgia

Access To Law, Inc.
420 South Peachtree Street, Norcross, GA 30071
770-685-1499
www.accesstolawfoundation.org

Catholic Charities of Atlanta
2305 Parklake Dr, NE, Suite 150, Atlanta, GA 30345
678-222-3920
www.catholiccharitiesatlanta.org

Hawaii

Catholic Charities Hawaii (Island of Hawaii Office)
202 Waianuenue Ave, Hilo, HI 96720
808-961-7030
1822 Keeaumoku Street, Honolulu, HI 96822
808-524-4673
www.catholiccharitieshawaii.org

Idaho

Catholic Charities of Idaho – Nampa Family Strengthening Center
847 Park Centre Way, Suite 7, Nampa, ID 83651
208-466-9926
www.ccidaho.org

Mountain States Group – Agency for New Americans
1614 W. Jefferson Street, Boise, ID 83702
208-338-0033
www.mtnstatesgroup.org/

DIRECTORY OF IMMIGRATION LEGAL SERVICES PROVIDERS

Illinois

Administer Justice
1750 Grandstand Pl, Suite 15, Elgin, IL 60123
847-780-7080
www.administerjustice.org

Catholic Charities of Chicago – Immigration and Naturalization Services
651 W. Lake Street, Chicago, IL 60661
312-427-7078
www.catholiccharities.net

Indiana

Catholic Charities Indianapolis – Immigration Legal Services
1400 N. Meridian Street, Indianapolis, IN 46202
317-236-1517
www.archindy.org/cc/refugee/index.html

Valparaiso Immigration Clinic
Valparaiso University Law School, Heritage Hall
510 Freeman Street, Valparaiso, IN 46383
219-465-7903
www.valpo.edu/law/current-students/c-academics/c-clinic-and-skill-based-learning/c-law-clinics

CHAPTER 27

Iowa

Immigrant Rights Network of Iowa
1111 9th St, Suite 380, Des Moines, IA 50314
515-974-5199
www.irnofiowa.org

Justice for Our Neighbors – Iowa
211 E. 3rd Street, Storm Lake, IA 50588
712-732-7783
www.iajfon.org

Kansas

Catholic Charities of Northeast Kansas – La Luz Center for Legal Assistance
2220 Central Ave, Kansas City, KS 66102
913-621-1504
www.catholiccharitiesks.org/

Catholic Charities of Wichita – Immigration & Refugee Services
437 N. Topeka Street, Wichita, KS 67202
316-264-0282
www.catholiccharitieswichita.org/

Kentucky

Catholic Charities of Louisville, Inc. – Immigration Legal Services
2911 S. 4th Street, Louisville, KY 40208
502-637-9786
www.cclou.org/

Kentucky Equal Justice Center – Maxwell Street Legal Clinic
Maxwell Street Legal Clinic
201 E. Maxwell Street, Lexington, KY 40508
859-233-3840
maxlegalaid.kyequaljustice.org/

Louisiana

Catholic Charities of New Orleans – Immigrant Survivors Service
1000 Howard Ave, 2nd Floor, New Orleans, LA 70113
504-310-8765
www.ccano.org

Central Louisiana Interfaith Immigration Center
PO Box 7417, Alexandria, LA 71302
318-445-6424, ext. 211
www.diocesealex.org

Maine

Catholic Charities Maine – Refugee and Immigration Services (Portland Office)
80 Sherman Street, Portland, ME 04101
207-523-2793
www.ccmaine.org/refugee-immigration-services

Immigrant Legal Advocacy Project
309 Cumberland Ave, Suite 201, Portland, ME 04101
207-780-1593
www.ilapmaine.org

CHAPTER 27

Maryland

Catholic Charities of Baltimore Immigration Legal Services, Esperanza Center
430 S. Broadway, Baltimore, MD 21231
410-534-8015
www.catholiccharities-md.org/immigrants/

Catholic Legal Immigration Network (CLINIC)
8757 Georgia Ave, Suite 850, Silver Spring, MD 20910
301-565-4800
https://cliniclegal.org/

International Rescue Committee
3516 Eastern Ave, Baltimore, MD 21224
410-327-1885
http://www.rescue.org

Justice for Our Neighbors
6201 Belcrest Rd, Hyattsville, MD 20782
301-927-6133

Massachusetts

Catholic Charities of Boston – Refugee and Immigration Services
275 W. Broadway, South Boston, MA 02127
617-464-8100
www.ccab.org/

The Political Asylum/Immigration Representation (PAIR) Project
98 North Washington Street, Suite 106, Boston, MA 02114
617-742-9296
www.pairproject.org/

Ascentria Care Alliance
51 Union St, Suite 222, Worcester, MA 01608
508-754-1121
http://www.ascentria.org

Michigan

Catholic Charities of Southeast Michigan
15945 Canal Rd, Clinton Township, MI 48038
586-416-1113 ext. 4019
www.ccsem.org

Justice for Our Neighbors-Southeastern Michigan
(Beverly Hills Office)
20000 W. 13 Mile Rd, Beverly Hills, MI 48025
734-709-1151
www.jfonsemi.org

Minnesota

Minnesota Advocates for Human Rights
330 Second Avenue South, Suite 800, Minneapolis, MN 55401 USA
612-341-3302
www.mnadvocates.org

Immigrant Law Center of Minnesota
450 North Syndicate Street, Suite 200 St. Paul, MN 55104
651-641-1011
www.ilcm.org/

Immigration Law Practice Group – University of St. Thomas
Interpersonal Center, 2115 Summit Ave, St. Paul, Minnesota 55105
651-962-4960

Mississippi

Catholic Charities of Jackson – Immigration Clinic
200 N. Congress Street, Suite 100, Jackson, MS 39201
601-948-2635
www.catholiccharitiesjackson.org

Mississippi Immigrants Rights Alliance
612 N. State Street, Jackson, MS 39202
601-354-9355 ext. 3
www.yourmira.org

Missouri

Interfaith Legal Services for Immigrants
4158 Lindell Blvd, St. Louis, MO 63108
314-371-4640
www.ilsilegal.org/

Legal Aid of Western Missouri
920 Southwest Blvd, Kansas City, MO 64108
816-474-9868
www.lawmo.org/

Migrant and Immigrant Community Action Project
9300 Olive Blvd., LL, St. Louis, MO 63132
314-995-6995
www.mica-project.org

DIRECTORY OF IMMIGRATION LEGAL SERVICES PROVIDERS

Montana

Border Crossing Law Firm
312 N Ewing Street, Helena, Mt 59601
406-594-2004
http://bordercrossinglaw.com/

Montana residents may also want to try the following organization in North Dakota:
Lutheran Social Services of North Dakota – Immigration Services
4720 - 7th Ave. S. Suite B, Fargo, ND 58103
701-235-7341
www.lssnd.org/newamericans/index.html

Nebraska

Justice for Our Neighbors Nebraska
2414 E Street, Omaha, NE 68107
402-898-1349
www.jfon-ne.org

Lutheran Family Services – Lutheran Immigration Services
1811 W. 2nd Street, Suite 365, Grand Island, NE 68803
308-382-4255
www.lfsneb.org/community/immigration.asp

CHAPTER 27

Nevada

Legal Aid Center of Southern Nevada
800 S. 8th Street, Las Vegas, NV 89101
702-386-1070
www.lacsn.org

Nevada Legal Services
650 Tahoe St., Reno, NV 89509
775-284-3491
www.nlslaw.net

New Hampshire

New Hampshire Catholic Charities – Immigration and Refugee Services
325 Franklin Street, Manchester, NH 03101
603-624-4717
www.nh-cc.org

New Jersey

American Friends Service Committee – Immigrant Rights Program (Newark Office)
89 Market Street, 6th Floor, Newark, NJ 07102
973-643-1924
http://afsc.org/program/immigrant-rights-program-newark-nj

Casa Esperanza
213 West Union Ave, Bound Brook, NJ 08805
732-748-1111
www.casaesperanzanj.com

Catholic Charities of the Archdiocese of Newark
590 North 7th Street, Newark, NJ 07107
973-596-4100
www.ccannj.com/index.php

New Mexico

New Mexico Immigrant Law Center
714 4th St S.W., Albuquerque, NM 87102
505-247-1023
http://nmilc.org

Catholic Charities of Las Cruces, Inc. – Legal Services Program
424 N. Downtown Mall, Suite 900, Las Cruces, NM 88001
575-203-1001
www.catholiccharitiesdlc.org/about/legal-services-program/

New York

African Services Committee
429 W. 127th Street, 2nd Floor, New York, NY 10027
212-222-3882
www.africanservices.org

Camba Legal Services
2211 Church Ave, Brooklyn, NY 11226
718-940-6311
www.camba.org

CHAPTER 27

Hebrew Immigrant Service Committee (HIAS)
333 Seventh Ave, 16th Floor, New York, NY 10001 - 5019
212-967-4100
www.hias.org/en

Journey's End Refugee Services
2495 Main St # 317, Buffalo, NY 14214
716-882-4963
www.jersbuffalo.org/

My Sisters' Place
One Water Street, White Plains, NY 10601
914-683-1333
http://mspny.org/

New York Immigration Coalition (NYIC)
(Can provide comprehensive referrals throughout NY State)
www.thenyic.org/home

Safe Horizon
Brooklyn, New York, NY
347-328-8110
www.safehorizon.org

USCRI Albany
991 Broadway #223, Albany, NY 12204
518-459-1790
www.refugees.org/about-us/where-we-work/albany/

DIRECTORY OF IMMIGRATION LEGAL SERVICES PROVIDERS

North Carolina

JusticeMatters
PO Box 61696, Durham, NC 27715
919-794-7511
http://justicemattersnc.org/

Legal Services of Southern Piedmont – Immigrant Justice Program
1431 Elizabeth Ave, Charlotte, NC 28204
704-376-1600
www.lssp.org

North Dakota

Lutheran Social Services of North Dakota – Immigration Services
4720 - 7th Ave. S. Suite B, Fargo, ND 58103
701-235-7341
www.lssnd.org/newamericans/index.html

Southern Minnesota Regional Legal Services, Inc. – Refugee, Immigrant, and Migrant Services (Fargo Office)
118 Broadway, Suite 616, Fargo, ND 58102
701-232-8872
www.smrls.org

Ohio

Community Legal Aid
11 Central Square, 7th Floor, Youngstown, OH 44503
330-983-2619
www.communitylegalaid.org/

Community Refugee and Immigration Services
1925 E. Dublin-Granville Rd, Suite 102, Columbus, OH 43229
614-235-5747
www.crisohio.org

Oklahoma

Catholic Charities of Oklahoma City – Immigration Assistance Program
1501 N. Classen Blvd, Oklahoma City, OK 73106
405-523-3001
www.catholiccharitiesok.org

YWCA Multicultural Center – Immigrant and Refugee Program
8145 E. 17th Street, Tulsa, OK 74112
918-663-0377
www.ywcatulsa.org

Oregon

Catholic Charities of Portland – Immigration Legal Services (Portland Office)
2740 S.E. Powell Blvd, Suite 2, Portland, OR 97202
503-542-2855
www.catholiccharitiesoregon.org

Immigration Counseling Service
519 S.W. Park Ave, Suite 610, Portland, OR 97205
503-221-1689
www.ics-law.org

DIRECTORY OF IMMIGRATION LEGAL SERVICES PROVIDERS

Pennsylvania

Catholic Social Services of Philadelphia – Immigration Program
227 North 18th Street, Philadelphia, PA 19103
215-854-7019
www.catholicsocialservicesphilly.org/immigration_services.php

HIAS Pennsylvania
2100 Arch St, 3rd Floor, Philadelphia, PA 19103
215-832-0900
www.hiaspa.org

Nationalities Service Center
1216 Arch Street, Philadelphia, PA 19107
215-893–8400
www.nationalitiesservice.org

Pennsylvania Immigration and Citizenship Coalition
http://paimmigrant.org/resources/legal-services

Pennsylvania Immigration Resource Center
112 Pleasant Acres Rd, Suite I, PO BOX 20339, York, PA 17402
717-600-8099
www.pirclaw.org

CHAPTER 27

Rhode Island

Catholic Charities of Providence – Office of Immigration and Refugee Services
1 Cathedral Sq, Providence, RI 02903
401-421-7833 ext. 129
www.dioceseofprovidence.org/?id=107

Dorcas International Institute of Rhode Island – Citizenship and Immigration Services
645 Elmwood Ave, Providence, RI 02907
401-461-5940
www.iiri.org/

South Carolina

Catholic Charities of the Piedmont
204 Douthit Street, Greenville, SC 29601
864-242-2233

South Carolina Legal Services (Florence Office)
320 S. Coit Street, Florence, SC 29501
843-413-9500
www.sclegal.org

South Dakota

Lutheran Social Services of South Dakota
705 East 41st Street, Suite 200, Sioux Falls, SD 57105
800-568-2401, or 605-357-0100
www.lsssd.org

Sisters of the Presentation of the Blessed Virgin Mary – Caminando Juntos
617 E. 7th Street, Sioux Falls, SD 57103
605-274-3735
www.presentationsisters.org

Tennessee

Community Legal Center
910 Vance Ave, Memphis, TN 38126
901-543-3395
www.clcmemphis.com

Tennessee Justice for Our Neighbors
5112 Raywood Ln, Hillcrest United Methodist Church, Nashville, TN 37211
615-823-1945
http://tnjfon.org

Texas

American Gateways (Austin Office)
314 E. Highland Mall Blvd, Suite 501, Austin, TX 78752
512-478-0546 ext. 200
www.americangateways.org

Boat People SOS (Houston Office)
11360 Bellaire Blvd., Suite 910, Houston, TX 77072
281-530-6888
www.bpsoshou.org

CHAPTER 27

Catholic Charities Dallas – Immigration and Legal Services
9461 LBJ Frwy, Suite 100, Dallas, TX 75243
214-634-7182
www.catholiccharitiesdallas.org

Casa Marianella
821 Gunter Street, Austin, TX 78702
512-385-5571
www.casamarianella.org

Las Americas Immigrant Advocacy Center
1500 E. Yandell Dr., El Paso, TX 79902
915-544-5126
http://las-americas.org

South Texas Pro Bono Asylum Representation Project (ProBAR)
301 E. Madison Avenue, Harlingen, TX 78550
956-425-9231

ProBAR Children's Project
119 W. Van Buren Avenue, Suite 204, Harlingen, TX 78550
956-365-3775
www.americanbar.org/groups/public_services/immigration/projects_initiatives/south_texas_pro_bono_asylum_representation_project_probar.html

Refugee and Immigrant Center for Education and Legal Services (RAICES)
1305 N. Flores St., San Antonio, TX 78212
210-226-7722
www.raicestexas.org

DIRECTORY OF IMMIGRATION LEGAL SERVICES PROVIDERS

Utah

Catholic Community Services of Utah – Immigration & Refugee Resettlement
745 E. 300 S, Salt Lake City, UT 84102
801-977-9119
www.ccsutah.org

International Rescue Committee
221 S 400 W, P.O. BOX 3988, Salt Lake City, UT 84110
801-328-1091
www.rescue.org

Vermont

Vermont Immigration and Asylum Advocates
241 N. Winooski Ave, Burlington, VT 05401
802-864-3200
www.vtimmigrationandasylum.org

Vermont Law School – South Royalton Legal Clinic
P.O. Box 117, 190 Chelsea Street, South Royalton, VT 05068
802-831-1500
www.vermontlaw.edu/x11480.xml

Virginia

Ayuda (Sterling Office)
46950 Community Plaza, Suite 213, Sterling, VA 20164
703-444-7009
www.ayuda.com

International Rescue Committee
609 E. Market Street, Suite 104, Charlottesville, VA 22902
434-979-7772
www.rescue.org

Northern Virginia Family Service
6400 Arlington Blvd, Suite 110, Falls Church, VA 22042
571-748-2806
www.nvfs.org

Washington (Washington State)

Northwest Detention Center Roundtable
621 Tacoma Ave South, Suite 501, Tacoma, WA 98402
nwdcr.info@gmail.com
http://nwdcroundtable.org
Meets at St. Leo's Church in Tacoma
710 S 13th St, Tacoma, WA 98405
www.stleoparish.org

Northwest Immigrant Rights Project (NWIRP) (Seattle Office)
615 2nd Ave, Suite 400, Seattle, WA 98104
206-587-4009
www.nwirp.org/

Lutheran Community Services Northwest – Refugee Program
115 N.E. 100th Street, Suite 200, Seattle, WA 98125
206-694-5700
www.lcsnw.org/services.html

Washington, D.C. (listed under "District of Columbia" above)

DIRECTORY OF IMMIGRATION LEGAL SERVICES PROVIDERS

West Virginia

Catholic Charities West Virginia – Migration & Refugee Services
1116 Kanawha Blvd E., Charleston, WV 25301
304-343-1036
www.catholiccharitieswv.org

Legal Aid of West Virginia
922 Quarrier Street, 4th Floor, Charleston, WV 25301
304-343-4481
www.lawv.net/

Wisconsin

Jewish Social Services of Madison
6434 Enterprise Ln, Madison, WI 53719
608-278-1808
www.jssmadison.org/

International Institute of Wisconsin
1110 N. Old World 3rd St, Suite 420, Milwaukee, WI 53203
414-225-6220
www.iiwisconsin.org

Wyoming

University of Wyoming College of Law – Legal Services Program
1000 E. University Ave, Department 3010, Laramie, WY 82071
307-766-2104
http://uwadmnweb.uwyo.edu/law/Student_life/Clinics/lglsrvs.asp

CHAPTER 28

Important Phone Numbers and Websites

Administration for Children and Families, U.S. Department of Health and Human Services:
www.acf.hhs.gov/

Search online to see what government programs and services are available to migrant populations, including victims of human trafficking, refugees, and survivors of torture.

American Civil Liberties Union:
212-549-2500, www.aclu.org
Call with questions or reports of civil rights abuses.

American Immigration Lawyers Association:
202-216-2400, www.aila.org
Call to get referrals to immigration lawyers, and see this website for the referral system: www.ailalawyer.com.

Office for Civil Rights and Civil Liberties (CRCL):
866-644-8360, www.dhs.gov/crcl

Call if your rights have been violated by DHS immigration enforcement or policy.

Detained Torture Survivors' Legal Support Network, Lutheran Immigration and Refugee Service:
410-230-2740, www.lirs.org
Call or search online for information about organizations that provide services for survivors of torture.

EOIR (Executive Office for Immigration Review; or Immigration Court): 800-898-7180
Call to find out the status of a case before the Immigration Court, or use EOIR's Free Legal Services Provider List (www.justice.gov/eoir/probono/states.htm) to find a lawyer in your state.

Emergency: 911
Call for help with a medical emergency, crime, or fire.

Florence Immigrant and Refugee Rights Project:
520-868-0191, www.firrp.org
Call or search online to get pro se materials, which will explain how you can represent yourself if you cannot find a lawyer or BIA accredited representative.

Immigration Law Help:
www.immigrationlawhelp.org
Search for an immigration lawyer in your state.

National Domestic Violence Hotline:
800-799-7233, 800-787-3224, www.thehotline.org
Call for help in 170 languages if you or your children are being abused by a partner or spouse.

IMPORTANT PHONE NUMBERS AND WEBSITES

National Human Trafficking Resource Center:
888-373-7888, www.polarisproject.org
Call for help with crisis intervention, urgent and non-urgent referrals, tip reporting, and comprehensive anti-trafficking resources.

National Lawyers Guild:
617-227-9727, www.nlg.org
Call to get referrals to immigration lawyers.

Office of Special Counsel for Immigration-Related Unfair Employment Practices:

- National Worker Information Hotline (employee): 800-255-7688
- National Employer Information Hotline (employer): 800-255-8155

Call with questions about your right to work. Call if your employer has questions about your right to work. www.justice.gov/crt/osc/

Social Security Administration (SSA):
800-772-1213, www.ssa.gov
Call with questions about applying for a Social Security number.

Supplemental Nutrition Assistance Program (SNAP):
800-221-5689, www.fns.usda.gov/snap
Call to get the number for your state food stamp program.

USCIS Form Request Hotline:
800-870-3676, www.uscis.gov/forms
Call to request USCIS forms for immigration benefits and immigration procedures. Also, call to find out where to send completed forms.

USCIS National Customer Service Center:
800-375-5283, www.uscis.gov
Call to find out the status of an immigration application.

GLOSSARY

A-number (Alien number)
An 8- or 9-digit number that starts with A and is written on all of your immigration documents. It is your personal identification number with Department of Homeland Security.

Affidavit of Relationship (AOR)
Part of the application for bringing family members through the P3 Family Reunification Program, which shows how you are related.

AR-11
USCIS form that you must file when you move; also known as an Alien's Change of Address Card.

Asylum seeker
Someone already in the U.S. or at a port of entry who is unable or unwilling to return to his or her country of origin because of persecution or a well-founded fear of persecution based on race, religion, nationality, membership in a particular social group, or political opinion; and whose government is unwilling or unable to

protect him or her. Unlike a refugee, an asylum seeker has not received permission to stay in the U.S. before arriving.

Asylee
Someone who was granted asylum in the U.S., either by a USCIS Asylum Officer, or by an Immigration Judge in court.

Board of Immigration Appeals (BIA)
The U.S. government body that reviews decisions of the immigration court (under the EOIR) on appeal. It also certifies organizations and individuals who hold expertise in immigration law, but are not lawyers, to answer certain legal questions and help fill out legal forms.

BIA accredited representative
An approved individual from a recognized agency that can help with certain immigration questions and forms, often at a lower cost than a lawyer.

Civil Rights Civil Liberties (CRCL)
The U.S. government agency that investigates complaints about unfair treatment or violation of civil rights in DHS policies or activities.

Civil Surgeon
A physician (doctor) approved by USCIS to conduct the medical examination of applicants seeking to adjust status to lawful permanent resident.

Convention Against Torture (CAT)
An international agreement that signatory countries will not return a person to a country where they are likely to be tortured. You can apply for relief to stay in the U.S. under CAT if you have been or believe you are likely to be tortured in your country.

GLOSSARY

Continued Presence (CP) certification
Permission from ICE to stay in the U.S. for one year to help law enforcement as a potential witness in a trafficking crime.

Cuban-Haitian entrant
An individual granted parole or other protective status designed for Cubans and Haitians, or a Cuban or Haitian who is in the U.S., not subject to a final order of removal, and is either in removal proceedings or has submitted an asylum application.

Customs and Border Protection (CBP)
The U.S. government agency that enforces immigration and customs laws primarily near international borders and at land, sea, and air international ports of entry.

Department of Homeland Security (DHS)
The federal agency responsible for offering immigration services and enforcing immigration laws. The most important divisions for immigration purposes are USCIS (U.S. Citizenship and Immigration Services), ICE (Immigration and Customs Enforcement), and CBP (Customs and Border Protection).

Department of Justice (DOJ)
The U.S. government agency that is responsible for enforcing U.S. law and administering justice. It contains the Executive Office for Immigration Review (EOIR), which contains the Immigration Court system and the BIA (Board of Immigration Appeals).

Department of Motor Vehicles (DMV)
The state office where you can get a state identification card or driver's license; name may vary depending on your state.

GLOSSARY

Employment Authorization Document (EAD)
Work permit, approved by USCIS.

Executive Office of Immigration Review (EOIR)
The U.S. government agency that oversees the immigration court system. It is part of the Department of Justice.

Final order of removal
A decision by an Immigration Judge or USCIS stating that a person must be deported to their country of origin, after removal proceedings have finished. Some people with a final order of removal remain under federal supervision because they cannot be deported to their country of origin.

Form 1099
A U.S. government form that states how much money you made during the year, and is used to file income tax every year with the U.S. government.

Freedom of Information Act (FOIA) request
U.S. government form that you or your lawyer can submit to ask for copies of your immigration and health records.

G-589
U.S. government form that describes the property taken from you when you were detained, including documents and cash.

G-884
U.S. government form that requests original documents from detention facilities or government agencies.

GLOSSARY

Green Card
Another name for the card that shows lawful permanent residence (LPR) status. Note: the card is no longer actually green!

I-9
A form your employer fills out that shows you have the appropriate documentation to work.

I-94
An identification card that shows proof of your status; also known as an Arrival-Departure Record. You should receive it when you enter the country as a refugee, and should have also received one if you were detained. It used to be a white card with a stamp that states your status; for example, "asylum granted indefinitely," or parole. However, in early 2013, some I-94s became electronic, and you may no longer receive a paper I-94. Instead, you can find your I-94 information by filling out the information on this website: www.cbp.gov/I94.

I-131
Application to travel outside the U.S. for certain immigrants who may be eligible to travel outside the U.S. and return.

I-485
Application form for Lawful Permanent Resident (LPR) status.

I-589
Application for Asylum and Withholding of Removal.

I-730
Refugee/Asylee Relative Petition; a USCIS form that allows refugees and asylees to petition to bring their spouse (husband or wife) and

unmarried children under age 21 to the U.S. (or apply for aslyee status if they are already in the U.S.).

ID

Identification, such as a state driver's license or other card with your photograph, name, and other important information that proves your identity.

Immigration and Customs Enforcement (ICE)

The U.S. government agency that carries out immigration and customs laws inside the U.S. and that oversees immigration detention and removal.

Immigration and Nationality Act (INA) of 1952

The law that, along with other immigration laws, treaties, and conventions of the U.S., addresses immigration, temporary admission, naturalization, or removal of non-citizens.

Individual Development Account (IDA)

A U.S. government program that matches money saved with government dollars; can be used for education, a car, a house, or other important investments.

Judge's order

A form that shows proof of your status; also called a court order or a court decision.

Lawful Permanent Residency (LPR)

Immigration status granted by DHS/USCIS that allows someone to live in the U.S. permanently (as long as they obey the law) and allows them to eventually naturalize (become a U.S. citizen) once they meet certain requirements.

GLOSSARY

Legal protective status
For the purposes of this manual, legal protective status means you have received some permission to stay in the U.S., temporarily or permanently.

Matching Grant Program
A U.S. government program that helps asylees and refugees find jobs and become able to support themselves within four to six months

Medicaid
A U.S. government program that allows certain eligible immigrants to visit doctors and hospitals and receive medical care at a low cost, subject to certain eligibility requirements.

Office of Refugee Resettlement (ORR)
A U.S. government office under the Administration for Children and Families that manages programs that provide economic, health, and social service assistance to the following groups: refugees, asylees, trafficking victims, survivors of torture, Unaccompanied Alien Children, SIV-holders from Iraq and Afghanistan, Cuban/Haitian entrants, and Amerasians.

Parolee
In this manual, a parolee only refers to someone who is allowed to enter the U.S. for humanitarian reasons but who could not apply as a refugee. (A person who is released from detention on parole with a final order of removal can also be called a parolee.)

Post office
An office that processes U.S. mail and sells money orders, calling cards, and stamps.

GLOSSARY

Processing fee
Money you need to send in with a USCIS form to apply for certain immigration benefits. You should check the USCIS website to be sure you are paying the correct amount by finding the form you had to submit here: www.uscis.gov/forms.

Proof of status
Any document, preferably issued by the U.S. government, which shows your immigration status in the U.S.

Public housing
Housing owned and operated by a public housing agency that can be rented by low-income people.

Refugee
Someone outside of his or her country of origin who is unable or unwilling to return because of persecution or a well-founded fear of persecution based on race, religion, nationality, membership in a particular social group, or political opinion; and whose government is unwilling or unable to protect him or her. Unlike an asylum seeker, a refugee is given permission to enter the U.S. before arriving.

Refugee Cash Assistance (RCA)
U.S. government program that provides financial assistance to childless refugee and asylee adults (and several other eligible immigrant groups) who have little money.

Refugee Medical Assistance (RMA)
U.S. government program that allows refugees and asylees (and several other eligible immigrant groups) to visit a doctor and get medical care at a low cost.

GLOSSARY

Return receipt
A postcard that informs you that a piece of mail was delivered. There is a fee for this post office service, but it is best to use this service when mailing immigration forms, so you can be sure they were received.

Social Security number (SSN)
An identification number used in the U.S. to work and study.

Special Immigrant Juvenile Status (SIJS)
A status given to eligible undocumented children considered a court dependent and eligible for long-term foster care who receive support from a federal program. It leads to lawful permanent resident (LPR) status.

Special Immigrant Visa (SIV)
Status given to eligible Iraqis and Afghanis who supported the U.S. military effort in their countries and are at risk because of their help. They are eligible for the same benefits as refugees and asylees.

SS-5
A form used to apply for a Social Security number.

Supplemental Nutrition Assistance Program (SNAP)
A U.S. government program that provides assistance to receive food for people in need (sometimes called Food Stamps Program).

Supplemental Security Insurance (SSI)
A U.S. government program that gives assistance to individuals who are blind, disabled, or age 65 or older and have limited income and resources.

GLOSSARY

T-visa
A visa that victims of human trafficking are able to apply for to gain legal protection to stay in the U.S. They are eligible for most of the same benefits as refugees.

Temporary Assistance for Needy Families (TANF)
A U.S. government program that provides financial assistance to some low-income families. Note: it usually has a different name in each state.

U-visa
A visa that victims of certain crimes are able to apply for if they are willing to help law enforcement investigate and prosecute the criminal case.

USCIS (U.S. Citizenship and Immigration Services)
The U.S. government office responsible for providing immigration services. It is part of the Department of Homeland Security.

VAWA (Violence Against Women Act)
A law that provides protection to victims of domestic violence, including allowing certain immigrant victims of domestic violence (spouses, children, or parents of a U.S. citizen; and spouses or children of an LPR/green card holder) to obtain their green cards without having to go through their U.S. citizen or LPR abuser.

W-2
A form that states annual income; used to file income tax with the U.S. government.

Withholding of Removal (WOR)
A USCIS order to prevent return of a person to their home country

if they have a well-founded fear of persecution based on race, religion, nationality, membership in a particular social group, or political opinion. It is a lesser form of protection than asylum, and does not lead to citizenship.

Women, Infants, and Children (WIC) Program
A U.S. government program that provides food and nutrition information to mothers, pregnant women, and children under 5 years old.

ACKNOWLEDGMENTS

First Steps has been brought to you by the Detained Torture Survivors' Legal Support Network, a program of LIRS's Access to Justice Unit. This publication was primarily researched, authored, and coordinated by Angela Edman, Staff Attorney for LIRS's Access to Justice (ATJ) program. Substantial portions of this publication were researched, authored, or coordinated by ATJ Training and Research Coordinator Julia Coffin, ATJ Program Fellows Justin Remer-Thamert and Nicholas Kang, ATJ Staff Attorney Megan Bremer, and Programs and Protection Administrative Assistant Sarah Vail. Angela Edman, Julia Coffin, Sarah Vail, and Children's Services Coordinator Kristine Poplawski co-authored the forthcoming status-specific supplements.

The following staff at LIRS edited this publication and provided expertise: ATJ Director Liz Sweet, Director for Community Integration Susan Gundlach, Assistant Director for Foster Care and Permanency Chak Ng, Administrative Assistant Sarah Vail, Senior Accountant Olga Butar, Project Coordinator for Network Engagement Laura Griffin, Assistant Director for Community Engagement Christine

Gedim, and ATJ Program Fellow Christina Andeweg.

Marketing and Communications Director Tara Mulder, Marketing Project Manager Clarissa Perkins, and Assistant Director for Online Communications Nicole Jurmo coordinated publication and marketing.

The Northeastern University School of Law Legal Skills in Social Context Social Justice Program provided legal research and writing in the initial stages of work. Many thanks to Faculty Supervisor Associate Dean for Experiential Education Luke Beirman; Research and Instruction Librarian Catherine Biondo; Advising Attorney Ilana Greenstein; Lawyering Fellows Angela Bunnell and Jillian Sadler; and law students Sally Barker, Mitali Biswas, Anastasia Butler-Carter, Molly Campbell, Jennifer Kim, Julianna Malogolowkin, Mado Martinez, Elizabeth McCarthy, Matthew Noonan, David Satin, Olivia Singer, Henry Tran, and Michelle Virshup.

Special thanks go to the following individuals, who provided invaluable expertise, edits, and ideas: Tanya Broder, Avideh Moussavian, and Linton Joaquin at the National Immigration Law Center; Casie-Lee Miller at Lutheran Social Services Northeast; Laura Burdick at Catholic Legal Immigration Network, Inc. (CLINIC); Shanti Martin at Kids In Need of Defense (KIND); Lindsay Jenkins at UNHCR; Elizabeth Yaeger at Hebrew Immigrant Aid Society (HIAS) Pennsylvania; Aleksander Milch at HIAS New Jersey; Annie Sovcik at the Center for Victims of Torture; Edna Yang at American Gateways; Daniel Stracka at Unitarian Universalist Refugee and Immigrant Services and Education; Sarah Ignatius at the PAIR Project; Rachel Winch at the Restoration Project; immigration attorneys Angela Eveler and Christina Powers; and especially Pat Hatch, founder and former Executive Director of FIRN (Foreign-born Information and Referral Network) and recent retiree from the

ACKNOWLEDGMENTS

Maryland Office for Refugees and Asylees. This manual would not have been what it is without your valuable support.

Many thanks to the refugees, asylum seekers, and former recipients of LIRS services who provided feedback for this publication. Particular thanks go to the residents of the Reservoir Hill House of Peace in Baltimore, MD for providing extremely helpful feedback and suggestions from the asylum seeker perspective.

We also wish to acknowledge the National Immigration Law Center, the National Immigration Project of the National Lawyers Guild, the ACLU's Immigrants' Rights Project, and USCIS for their wealth of resources that informed this guide.

We wish to thank the U.S. Department of Health and Human Services, Administration for Children and Families, Office of Refugee Resettlement, which generously funds LIRS's Detained Torture Survivors' Legal Support Network (DTS). The DTS Network is a nationally led, locally implemented consortium of legal service organizations that offers critical information, legal representation, and holistic services to protect torture survivors from removal and initiate the healing process. *First Steps* was funded in part through DTS funds, and in part through general LIRS funds.

LIRS encourages the printing and distribution of this guide. Information in this manual may be reprinted with the following note: Reprinted with permission of the Detained Torture Survivors' Legal Support Network, a program of Lutheran Immigration and Refugee Service.

Printed in 2014

CPSIA information can be obtained at www.ICGtesting.com
Printed in the USA
BVOW06s1553140915

417693BV00004B/5/P

9 780990 868941